Let's Illustrate

The Whys and Hows of Illustrating a Sermon

Eldon Weisheit

CPH
SAINT LOUIS

Copyright © 1998 Concordia Publishing House
3558 S. Jefferson Avenue, St. Louis, MO 63118-3968
Manufactured in the United States of America

Library of Congress Cataloging-in-Publication Data

Weisheit, Eldon
    Let's illustrate : the whys and hows of illustrating a sermon / Eldon Weisheit.
        p.   cm.
    ISBN 0-570-05331-5
    1. Preaching. 2. Homiletical illustrations. I. Title.
BV4226.W45   1998
251'.08—dc21   98-24656

1 2 3 4 5 6 7 8 9 10   07 06 05 04 03 02 01 00 99 98

Contents

Preface

For a Christian sermon, the medium is not the message. If it is Christian, the message must be grace. The methods we use to preach the message of God's grace in Jesus Christ will vary, but the methods dare never replace the message. In London, there is an annual "Preach Off" to select the best preacher in town. The judges do not consider the intent of the message, but rather the effectiveness of delivering the message. I would rather preach or hear a sermon that included the Gospel but would flunk Public Speaking 101, than to preach or hear a Christless sermon that won the "Preach Off."

However, such an effective message also deserves effective methods of preparation and delivery. Because we preach the Gospel is not an excuse for poor preparation or delivery. I think it might be heresy to make the resurrection of Christ from the dead either dull or obscure. Just as the Gospel must not be lost in flashy literary and oratorical styles, it must not be hidden in vague words and poor communication.

The message of the Gospel must always come via a medium. Look at the media that God himself uses to bring the Gospel to us. His Son became human. The incarnation of Christ uses humanity as a medium to deliver God's grace. When the Word became flesh (John 1:14), the medium became the message: God was and is with us.

God speaks to us through the Scriptures to tell us how he planned our salvation, how it happened, and how it applies to our lives today. The Bible is the medium we use to learn and to teach God's will and his ways.

The Holy Spirit works through people to pass the message from person to person, from generation to generation. We who believe become a part of God's media team. Many will not read the Scripture to meet Jesus Christ; but they will see and hear the message through us.

God's method of using a great diversity of people to spread his message works because he wants that message to go to a diverse world. From the specialized worldwide ministry of people such as Billy Graham, to parents who teach their children about Christ, to the neighbor who shows and speaks the Gospel in daily life, all use a variety of ways to share the same message.

This book is written for a small group within the large community of Christian communicators—the parish pastors. It is for those who preach to people with whom they also share the other experiences of Christian fellowship such as study, administration, worship, Christian service, and all the other functions of ministry in a local congregation. This book is for those who preach sermons that are a part of a dialog in the congregation including social events, pastoral calls, weddings, funerals, meetings, and all the other activities which bring people together in Christ's name.

As I was putting the last touches on this book, my wife and I had the opportunity to worship at Westminster Abbey in London on Christ the King Sunday. The preacher's message of our sin and God's grace in Christ was powerful and its effect on me lasting. There must have been 800 people at the worship service. The woman next to me said she was one of about 10 present who were members of the congregation—according to her count. Then I understood why one of my sermons would have been inadequate for that setting. I also realized the sermon I appreciated there would not have worked in the congregation where I am a member. The point of the story is that each one of us who preach has a very special task. There is no "preach off"

6

to find the best preacher. We all have to same message to be delivered to different people in different circumstances.

In this book, I offer many uses of media to preach the message of Christ. Many of the media come from my own experience and many I have received from others. None of the methods are guaranteed ways to get the Gospel out to all people. Each idea can be helpful to some preachers in some situations—and each could be disastrous in the wrong situation. It is your job to find the best resources that help you in your congregation.

Let me give you one more illustration about preaching. Suppose you were in charge of curriculum development at a seminary. You must combine homiletics with another department for the total education of pastors. With what other discipline would you put preaching?

Some would say homiletics and exegetical studies go together because a sermon must be built on God's Word. Others would say preaching is a part of dogmatics. Each sermon must be a part of the total body of Christian doctrine. The study of preaching could be included in liturgical studies because the sermon is given in a total worship context. Some might offer good reasons to include sermons under the educational department. Others might see it as a part of counseling. All of the above are good possibilities and show that preaching is a cross-discipline experience.

I would put homiletics with Pastoral Care (or Pastoral Theology). When pastors start working in a new congregation, their first contact with most people is through the sermon. Throughout their time in a parish their most regular opportunity to reach people is through the sermon. By the attitudes, priorities, and concerns they show in sermons, they establish the agenda for their entire ministry. In no way am I saying that preaching is the most important part of congregational ministry. Instead, I am saying that preaching is an important part of the entire ministry.

As a person who now sits in the pew, I would rather have a good pastor who is not such a good preacher, than a good preacher who is not such a good pastor. I'm glad I don't have to make that choice, and neither do the people in your congregation. Pastors care about and care for their people. That love is seen and heard in sermons.

Eldon Weisheit
Tucson, Arizona

CHAPTER 1

Why Preach This Sermon?

This book is about sermons and sermon illustrations. The first question is Why? Not, why use illustrations? That comes later. The question is not about sermons in general. We will not search history to find why sermons are almost always included in the Christian worship agenda. The question asks why you will preach the sermon you are working on now, and the one following that.

On Palm Sunday, I was a guest in a church where a dramatic reading of Christ's passion from *The Message* was used in the sermon slot. A member I knew said, "I'm sorry you didn't get to hear one of our pastor's sermons." I thought the reading was a sermon and I appreciated it, but I also heard murmuring in the parking lot. People expected a sermon.

You also expect to preach a sermon. It's in your job description. Why?

Let me illustrate the importance of this question by a story—the story that first made me ask why I preached (and published) sermons.

My denomination started building a national staff in the late 1940s. Each new department started producing materials for local congregations. As the number of boards increased, the cost of mailing all their material zoomed. Someone had a great idea. Start a magazine (later called *Advance*). Each department at the denominational headquarters would get two free pages each month to pass on material to their corresponding committee in congregations. *Advance Magazine* was a success. I appreciated it in my early ministry.

Fast forward to the 1970s. I was nominated to be the editor of *Advance*. I declined (as did everyone else) because it did not seem like a full-time job. Later I became the part-time, acting editor of *Advance*. I correctly understood my title meant I was the director of hospice for sick magazines. I soon discovered the problem. My biggest job was to nag each department head to give me two pages of material each month. The magazine was a success when the writers thought, "Here's my chance to help equip parish leaders for ministry." The magazine became terminally ill when the attitude changed to "Oh, no, it's not that time of the month again. Call me back tomorrow. I'll have something for you."

Do you preach because you have a message for those who hear, or because there is a time slot that has to be filled in the worship services?

WHO ANSWERS THE QUESTION?

Before we go any further, let me tell you how I see you and ask you to think about how you see me. I see you as a working pastor who has lots to do other than prepare sermons. I've been there, but now I'm retired. I still work at things like this, and I have a part-time job working on a product to be published on CD-ROM which will provide a Sunday-by-Sunday resource for pastors like you. So I spend at least two days a week studying the lessons for one day of the church year, then write and collect resources to offer to people like you. That means you and I are both working on sermons. I have more time, but I don't preach the sermons. You have less time, but you do the preaching. So I'm writing this book as a spin-off of the other project, as another way to do my ministry by helping you do yours. I tell you this so you know I know I'm only blowing in the wind unless I can offer you something that will help you next Sunday.

I see you as a pastor with multiduties. Some of the things on your To Do list can be delayed, but sermons must be done on schedule. You can cancel a meeting, but you can't phone everyone in the congregation and tell them worship services have been postponed this week because you aren't ready. So I'm your assistant pastor—the part-time, retired kind who disappears everytime he gets a chance for a cheap airline ticket. So every once in a while we meet for coffee or lunch—you're treating because you paid for this book. We talk about sermons—in this case especially illustrations. I don't see myself as an expert to tell you how to preach—remember I'm the assistant. But I can ask you questions about your preaching. Your thinking about the questions will probably be the best help I can give you. However, I also want to offer you some of my experience and my gift of creativity to the degree that the Holy Spirit gives it to me and transfers it to you. Most of all, I want to encourage you to follow your instincts on communication. In my early ministry a few people helped free me to communicate my way rather than the prescribed way. I'd like to do the same for you.

Since this is a book on illustrations, I'll illustrate the above. In England the people on the evening news are called readers because they read the news reports gathered and written by journalists. In our country we have a debate about those who work the news beat. Are they journalists who search for news and report it? Or, are they readers who use other people's material? I do not want to be a journalist who searches the Scripture and the hearts of people to write material for you to read. You are the journalist who may use my material, along with others, to search out the news of Scripture for the people who tune you in. In this analogy I am your research assistant.

So the above excursion was like the time-out while we gave our lunch orders, and I repeat my question to get us back on track. Why do you preach each week? You've had a little time to think about it, and you come up with your answer. This is nothing new. You've had to deal with it. But I want you to think about your answer. I preach because ….

YOUR VIEW OF YOUR SERMONS

As you explain why you preach, don't give an ought-to-be answer. Think about your sermons for the last month and give a what-really-happens answer. You have 18 minutes to preach at each service. For the time being, think of it as those two pages in *Advance Magazine*. Are you eager to fill your two pages? Have you got a message that demands more time? Are you using the time available for the message that is most important to you and to your congregation? Or, is your unspoken attitude "Is it that time of the week already?"

Below is a list of subjects that might be included in sermons. This is just a starter-set of ideas. Some of them may not seem important to you, or I may have forgotten a subject that is very important to you. Your assignment is to think about what you have to put into those 18 minutes next Sunday.

First go through the list and ask yourself if these are the reasons that you need to preach sermons. Think about the sermons you have preached recently and the one you are working on now. Then rate each item according to how often these items are in your sermons. The idea is to rate them by what you do, not what you should do.

E for every sermon.

R for regularly

F for frequently

O for occasionally

S for sometimes

N for never

I have tried to word each item objectively, but that is always difficult. If you need to change the wording of any topic, no problem.

All people need to attend public worship regularly.
Prayer is a part of our daily lives.
We need to share our faith with others.
All people are sinners.
Jesus died to pay for all sins.
The Bible is true.
The priesthood of all believers.
Beware of false prophets.
Jesus is both God and human.
The office of the ministry.
Believers will use their time, ability, and money to serve Christ.
God wants all people to be saved.
We must worship in the proper way.
Baptism and the Lord's Supper are means of grace.
Bible study is necessary.
Judgement Day is coming.
We need to know and believe true doctrine.
We must support the church at large.
We cannot divide the body of Christ.
We all have spiritual gifts.
We must separate ourselves from those who have false doctrine.
God can heal our illnesses.
Christ rose from the dead so we will also.
God is sovereign.
Millennium, tribulation, and rapture.

After you have added to the list and marked them according to the above system, evaluate your own results. Do the results reflect your own faith? Did you become a pastor to teach the things high on your list now? Have your priorities in preaching changed over the years? Does your list reflect the public doctrine of your denomination? Do you see anything in your preaching that would make your sermons different from other pastors in your denomination? different from other denominations? Does your list show you have a magnificent obsession? Does your list show you have an ax to grind?

AMONG YOUR PEERS

Let's assume you have been asked to preach a sermon at some gathering of other pastors in your denomination. Look at the list above again. Would you have different priorities when preaching to pastors than you do when preaching to your congregation? Most sermons that I hear at clergy groups start off with variations of "I'm nervous about preaching to my fellow preachers." Let it go! I need a sermon that is addressed to Eldon, sinner, believer, husband, father, son, citizen, church member, and yes, pastor.

Recently, I visited a congregation served by a pastor whom I had heard preach at pastors' conferences. I thought he was rather rigid, formal and … boring. However, in his congregation he was exciting and spiritual. The love of Christ was not just one point in his sermon—it showed up in his entire message. He had something he wanted to say to his congregation. His sermon was not long, but I had the feeling he would have a lot more to say if I came back next week. He filled the time when he preached at the conference.

I have asked you to think about sermons at clergy gatherings as you evaluate the purpose of your own preaching because you need to learn from the pros. Whether you are the speaker or the listener at such an event, you can learn more about your own preaching. By our training, and when we are with other pastors, we tend to evaluate sermons on scales left over from the grades given in classrooms. We want to preach good sermons, and we admire others who preach them. We want to avoid bad sermons, and we criticize those who preach them.

Over the years I have given up evaluating sermons (my own and those preached by others) on the good to bad scale. At least I try to. Instead, I want to preach and I want to hear *effective* sermons. Sermons are effective when they connect the Word of God to real life. It is unfortunate that pastors do not get to hear many sermons preached to congregations. Those who have another preaching pastor on staff have an advantage because they hear a sermon applied to a congregation. They can learn to evaluate how effective the sermon was.

During 32 of my 35 years as a pastor, I both preached sermons to congregations and wrote sermons for publication. I found out there is a big difference between the two ways to prepare a sermon. To me, the preached sermon is a much more spiritual assignment. It is what Jesus told us to do before he exited stage up. When I preach to a congregation, I am on the front line of God's service. When I write for publication, I am part of the support troops. The sermons I write (or this book) become effective only if they help those on the front line to be effective.

Frequently, I have people tell me they used my children's sermon books but, with a note of apology in their voices, they say they have changed them. I respond, "Thank God! When I preach them, I change them too." An embarrassing moment for me: Years ago I visited a church and was glad to see that the bulletin listed "Children's Sermon." They were rare in those days. My ego soared when the pastor walked out with one of my books in hand. My ego nose-dived when he held the suggested object in the other hand and read my sermon word for word.

One pulpit problem is too many pastors are still preparing sermons to please the ghosts of homiletics profs from the past and ecclesiastical overseers of the present. Both groups are in the same category as I am—we are all your assistants. You do not prepare your sermon to impress us. We are trying to impress you so you will use our material. Your sermon is for your congregation. The test of effectiveness does not come from your judgment about your sermon or from the reputation as a preacher you have among your peers. Your sermon is effective if it brings God's message to your people. That brings us to the next evaluation.

WHAT DO THE PEOPLE IN THE PEW HEAR?

Dr. Martin Mueller was my boss at *The Lutheran Witness* for about four years in the 1970s. I still like to find ways to thank him for the help he gave me in communication. This is one way I can say thank you again to him. He said if you listen to a pastor preach a sermon for three weeks in a row, you will know what his priorities are. I've learned to listen to sermons (and other communications) that way. What is the speaker (or writer) excited about? Why is the person doing the talking or writing, delivering this subject to this group of people?

If your sermons are going to be effective, they must affect those who hear them. Look back to the list (pp. 12–13) and the system I asked you to use to evaluate your sermons. How do you think your parishioners would rate the sermons they hear? How would that compare to the rating you gave the sermon you preached?

Recognize that the playing field has been totally changed. In the first place, you have been taught the art of preaching. You judge it by whatever standards you accepted for a sermon. Your evaluation, and that of the peer group, is professional. The members of your congregation take it personally, as well they should. They may miss something you had in the sermon because they come to hear God's Word, they may also receive something that you didn't give—but the Word gave.

When I started developing some of my own ideas about communication, I was serving a congregation with a little over 200 people in the two services each Sunday. One Sunday I tried something that just didn't work. I was so embarrassed about my flop I didn't want to stand at the door after the services. I was afraid people would tell me how bad the sermon was. But they didn't. That worried me, because many of the members had a feeling of ownership about sermons and freely offered help. I wondered why they didn't tell me I had preached a bad sermon. Weren't they listening?

The next week I worked and worked on the sermon. It came off great. As I walked to greet the people, I thought, "Billy Graham, eat your heart out!" The following week a couple from church invited my wife and me to dinner for what we had learned to call and appreciate as a "benefit." Other guests were invited so we could talk about Jesus.

During the meal the hostess gave the straight line, "I don't know how I'd get through the week if I didn't go to church. I still think about the sermon two weeks ago and it helps me."

I felt a chill as I remembered the bad sermon. So I said, "I think you mean last week (the outstanding sermon)."

"No," she said, "I can't remember last week's, but I'll never forget the one two weeks ago."

That event helped me get over the good/bad approach to sermons. From a homiletical point of view the first sermon was still a C- and the second one an A+. But the friend was not interested in homiletics. She was interested in Jesus and wanted to share her faith with her friends. The bad sermon was effective. Sorry about the good one.

That brings us to the second reason why the playing field is different when your church members evaluate your sermons than when you examine your own. There's one of you. How many of them? Each one has different needs and different expectations from sermons. There is no way you can please each person; you'll drive yourself into selling insurance if you try. But you can be effective for all. When we finally get to the "ways" of illustrations (and we will), one important issue will be variety. The same message needs to be delivered in a variety of ways so it can be understood and applied by all the members. Maybe you won't reach each person each week, but move your methods around and you'll get all but the most hard-hearted.

When you are trying to evaluate your church members' evaluations of your sermons, forget the that-was-a-good-sermon comments at the door. I've had people tell me I preached a good sermon after a service in which I led the worship and someone else preached. Listen to what people say as they leave church, but take it with a grain of salt. The after-church comment I remember most came from a 10-year-old boy in a church where I was a guest preacher. He said, very loudly, "You're not nearly as bad as most of them!" His mother was about to break several commandments over his head until I rescued him and thanked him.

The fact that you're reading this book indicates to me you are brave enough to admit you also haven't learned everything yet. The "also" means I am in the category. You have to be very brave to try the next step—but I encourage you to give it a go.

Make copies of the list and the evaluation code on pages 12–13. Have people who hear your sermons regularly evaluate you by the same system you evaluated yourself. In all cases explain the purpose and point out the end of the list where they may add more subjects. Pay special attention to anything that is added. Some ways to try:

Use this tool for a board of elders meeting—or in some congregations the church council. Explain that worship, at least the way many people define it, is an act of participation. People don't sit in the pew as an audience, they are participants. The sermon is a part of the worship service, and you need their participation. Ask the board members to participate in the sermons by giving you an evaluation. Mention they should not sign their names—even if they want to do so.

Use the evaluation tool in a Bible class—especially one that meets after the members have attended worship and heard the sermon.

Write a cover letter for the list, give it to selected members of the church, and ask them to return it.

If your bravery borders on heroism, put the list and cover letter in the parish newsletter and send it to everyone. This, of course, lets people who rarely or never hear your sermons evaluate them, and many will do so. What they say will have little to do with your sermons, but they will react to the sermons they heard years ago.

You need to remember, and you need to remind anyone who participates in this evaluation, that this is not a public opinion poll to decide what subjects need to be included in future sermons. I am encouraging the use of creativity in preaching, but that creativity does not include the message itself. The message has already been given to us; you're looking for the best way to deliver that message in a usable form.

Review time: First, I asked you to identify the purpose of your preaching. In this section I am offering ways for you to find out if the message you think is important is being heard as important by those who hear you. You need to know if you are sending mixed signals to the people in the pews. Let me put up some yellow lights to caution you about certain dangers.

I have heard sermons (and may have preached a few) that would have been good Law/Gospel sermons on paper. They spoke of our guilt and of God's grace through Jesus Christ. However, when the sermons were preached, the pastor got very excited about the Law. He put his passion into that part and then added the Gospel in a tone that said, "By the way, Jesus died for you so you are forgiven." The people who hear you will listen to your body language as much as your verbal language.

Do you have a pet peeve or pet project that shows up often in your sermons? All of us can do this without being aware of it. We've got to be friendlier. We need to sing louder. Please be quiet when you come into church. More people should attend congregational meetings. Each of these things may have a place—but not in the sermon. You are there to preach to the people's needs. Make sure that you are not preaching to your needs.

Do you use the sermon as a PR opportunity? I know the worship service reaches more members than any other means of communication in the congregation. But do a priority study on the needs of people. I was a visitor in a worship service where everything the pastor said involved taking door hangers with a message to the neighborhood. It was in his announcements, his introduction to the lessons, the sermon, and the prayers. I needed to be encouraged to share my faith in Christ with others, but that should have been the point of all the talk-talk. Then, "By the way, one way to share your faith would be to take these door hangers out to the neighborhood. Look at what they say." It's easy to talk about methods and lose the message.

Finally, and most important, your sermons are a part of a much larger communication network in your congregation. The people hear you talk at parties, meetings, and all the other places where two or three of you gather together. Do you show the same priorities outside of the pulpit as from it?

Recently, I attended a lecture given by a member of the Jesus Seminar. He was an excellent speaker, and I could learn verbal skills from him. He made it clear he did not believe that Jesus was God's Son in any way other than that we are all God's children. He knew Jesus died, but not in the way or for the reason described in the New Testament. His strongest statement of faith was that he did not believe Jesus rose from the dead.

During the question period someone asked him, "What is your imperative in life?" For the first time, that master speaker faltered. He started several sentences without completing them, then said something about existentialism.

I thought of the funeral sermon I had preached a few weeks before and the sermon I would preach the following Sunday. My imperative was clear in my mind and heart. I don't think those who heard my message wondered why I preached those sermons.

What is your imperative?

WHERE DOES THE MESSAGE COME FROM?

When I started preaching on a weekly basis, I worried I would run out of material in a few years. What more could I say on Christmas Eve? What would my message be on Easter morning in the year that I celebrated 10 years in the ministry? How many more times could I preach a sermon about grace, repentance, love?

During the last three years of my parish ministry I had the opposite concern. As I would look at the three lessons listed for that Sunday in the three-year lectionary, I would think, "This is my last chance to preach on these texts to people who see me as their pastor." After 35 years I had only scratched the surface of God's message for us in the Scripture.

The change in attitude from the alpha to the omega parts of my ministry came because my understanding of Scripture changed. I also started with the faith that the Bible is God's Word, inspired by the Holy Spirit. I still believe that. However, I also started with an attitude that God had given me the truth of Scripture and my job was to defend that truth and pass it on.

But as I worked with Scripture, I found it did a lot better job of defending itself than I could. So I decided I would teach the Scriptures rather than argue about them. But even more important, I discovered the more I used the message of the Bible, the more creative I became. Paul explains it in the fourth chapter of his second letter to the Corinthians. We who teach the Bible are just clay pots, and sometimes we are cracked pots—that's psycho-ceramics. But God works through us as long as we use his Word. We know his Word has power. He said, "Let there be light," and megawatts appeared. Now he tells us the same God has made his light shine in our hearts to bring us the knowledge of his glory shining in the face of Christ—that's verse 6. It took the same power of God that turned on the lights in the universe to turn the lights on in us. But it happened—and it happens!

Someone who had read my one book of poetry asked if I thought it was inspired. I said, "Yes, with second degree inspiration." When I read Scripture, I receive first degree inspiration. I believe the same Holy Spirit who inspired the authors who wrote, also inspires the readers that read. The Holy Spirit works on both ends of the God-human communication model. When we are exposed to first degree inspiration, we are inspired in the second degree. We pass the message on, but the power does not come from our intellect, our creativity, or our sincerity. It comes from the God who said, "Let the light shine!"

I think we can also speak of a third degree of inspiration for those who hear our message, but I start getting uncomfortable the more degrees we get away from the power source. Too many extension cords may lead to a power loss. But the extension cords are needed to get the message of the Gospel out to the edges and to lead people back to first degree inspiration.

You can be inspiring to others only when you have been inspired. The need to produce at least one sermon a week demands that you have a renewable source of inspiration. Listen to others who preach, in person or on the media, and identify what lights their fires. Where are they looking for inspiration? Now listen to your own sermons. What lights your fire to preach? Your best statement on the authority of Scripture will not be in a sermon about the subject, but when you show the power of Scripture each time you preach. You need to read others' books, listen to other speakers, take continuing education courses, but the Bible is your source of inspiration for your sermons.

All of us will occasionally have preacher's block. It's a blessing because it shows we are running on empty and need to be filled again. We can't give what we don't have. May I suggest two ways (not as either/or, but as both/and) to deal with preacher's block.

First, spend time alone with the text. This is not study time with commentaries and lexicons; it is not time to dig deep for hidden meanings in the text. Instead, just learn the text in simple English. Read it in several translations—I sometimes use as many as 12. Read each one to get another view of the text. Keep reading until you can tell the message of the text in your own words. Think of how you would tell it to a child, to a lifelong church member, to someone who just started attending church.

Next treatment for preacher's block: Close the books and turn off the computer. Go make some calls. Talk to someone who is angry and has left the church. Visit someone who is dying. Spend time with someone who has had no Christian training. Keep a few other people on your prospect list who have special needs. We pastors can often get so tied up in administration, special programs, denominational responsibilities, theological discussions, and other parts of our reality that we forget our purpose. Talking with people who need the message of Scripture helps us reorient our ministry. Think of the people you call on as representatives of others who will be in church, but who have not revealed their needs to you.

Then with both Scripture and the needs of people on the same program in your heart, you are ready to work on your sermon again.

An illustration for you: Remember what happens when you ride on an airplane. You sit down beside someone. Sometimes you nod to each other. Sometimes you speak. Sometimes you introduce yourselves by name. Sometimes you get involved in a conversation. Think about the differences. Why do you get deeply involved with one seatmate and totally ignore another? Some reasons:

You find you have something in common. You do the same kind of work, belong to the same church, or were born in the same town.

Some problem develops. The attendant spills coffee on both of you. Bad weather causes the plane to change destinations.

You have the same need. Both going to visit a sick parent. Both have the same illness. Both have lost a job.

You have the same joys. Look at the picture of my grandchild. We are going to vacation in the same place.

Now place two chairs side-by-side as though they were airplane seats. Place the text of the sermon you are preparing in one of the seats. This text is your friend because you have studied it for yourself and you know the message it gives. Then in your imagination, put the people who are to hear your sermon in the other seat. They are also your friends. You know many, if not all of them. Even the visitors come because they are looking for something and are hoping they can find it in the congregation you serve.

The sermon is easy—introduce your friends to each other. Look for messages in the text and experiences in the lives of the people who will hear your sermon. Find the matches. Glance again through the above list of reasons why people talk to each other on a plane. For your sermon you have an advantage: The text and the listeners will not be strangers in many cases. But here is a chance for them to talk to one another and to get better acquainted.

Take one of my airplane stories as an illustration: My wife and I were flying into New York City. The passenger to my right was an army master sergeant—and looked the part. A polite hello was all the conversation he needed. However, in front of us were two young Unitarian clergymen who enjoyed sharing a conversation over the seatback.

As we neared the airport, we hit rough weather. The pilot announced that it would be dangerous to land so he would look for another airport. After about 10 minutes of circling, the pilot announced that of all the options available our original destination was the best. We all remembered that he had told us it would be dangerous and were silent as the plane headed down through heavy turbulence and at last bounced on the runway. One of the men in front of us turned back and said, "Well, I guess it wasn't so bad. They didn't call on us to pray." The master sergeant said, "At times like that I don't depend on a middleman."

WHAT'S YOUR MESSAGE?

Early in my ministry a woman told me this story: She grew up in the church and her faith in Christ was an important part of her life. She married a man who had no Christian training. They talked about their differences and he said he would be willing to study her faith. She showed her husband a church bulletin that announced the beginning of a new class to study Christian doctrine. He went to the first class.

The pastor started the first class by holding up a Bible and saying, "This is God's Word. It is inspired by God and is without error. Unless you believe that, there is no reason for you to be here." Her husband got up and walked out—and never went back to church. He never learned the message in the Bible.

Her story influenced my ministry—including this book. Those of us who preach and teach the Christian message must clearly see in our own minds the difference between the source of the message and the communication of the message. Our job is to teach the truth of the Bible, not that the Bible is true. So you don't worry about me (at least on this subject), I believe the Bible is true. But if my main message is that the Bible is true, then I am communicating about communication. The Bible is God's communication to us. We love and proclaim the message—not the messenger.

Let's work with this idea. The authority of the message comes from God. He communicates that authority to us through Scripture; therefore the Scripture has authority. Apply this to the two major themes of the Bible—Law and Gospel.

The Bible tells us God's Law, such as Exodus 20 when God speaks the Ten Commandments and Matthew 5–7 when Jesus starts his ministry with his "State of the Law" address. God's Law is a part of his message throughout the Bible.

25

Many people will disagree with minute points of the Law in the Bible. Because they find fault with one legal detail, they throw the entire case out of court. Their argument is with the Bible. We dare not fall into the trap of defending the Bible; rather, our job is to refer the combatants back to God. The purpose of Scripture is to communicate God's message to us. We can't get sidetracked by communication-is-the-problem arguments and miss the reason the Law has authority. To put it simply, note the difference in the following: "The Bible tells us not to kill." "God tells us not to kill." Both are true and both are proper. The first uses a secondary source. The other uses a primary source.

The Bible also tells us the Good News that Jesus Christ is our Savior. We can teach this idea two ways. We can proclaim the Bible is true and all who believe its message will be saved. Then people can go read the Bible, find the Gospel and believe it. It works. Or, we can teach the message of Scripture; "Jesus Christ died to pay for your sins and rose from the dead to give you eternal life." Jesus Christ is the source of our salvation—that is, it comes from him. The Scripture is the means of grace—it is the method the Holy Spirit uses to bring the message to us.

Let me illustrate: A house is on fire. A fire hydrant is one block away. Firemen connect a hose to the fire hydrant and extinguish the fire. The question: Which put out the fire? The water or the hose? A hose will not put out a fire; in fact, a hose will burn. The water put out the fire. However, the hose was necessary because it was the means of getting the water from the fire hydrant to the fire.

You and I are sinners. Almost 2,000 years ago Christ destroyed the power of sin and death by his own death and resurrection. The Bible brings that message across the years and the miles to our lives today. How are we saved? By the Bible or by Christ? Christ is the one who has saved us. He is the source of our salvation. The Bible is the means the Holy Spirit uses to bring the message to us. Both are necessary, but each is necessary for different reasons. Christ is necessary because he is the only one who has dealt with our sin and our death. Others have told us how to live, but only Jesus has lived, died, and lived again for us. The Bible is necessary because it is the way the message of Christ comes to us—and it is the way we pass the message on to others.

If you regard your assignment, as I do mine, to preach the Bible, you do not preach about the Bible, but you proclaim its message. Many people who claim they believe the Bible is inspired by God and is without error teach different and even opposing messages from the sacred book. Do not use your sermon time to debate others—especially those not present. Instead, in your own mind, identify what you regard as the theme of the entire Bible.

Teaching Scripture is an important part of your preaching duties. When you teach, you ask the students to learn something that is either new or a development of what they already know. In most cases that requires change. Teach in a way that does not create a debate between those who disagree (or don't understand) with you or your denomination. Do not give your conclusion in a way that the listeners must either agree or disagree with you. Instead, offer the facts and options from Scripture and show what led you to your decision.

Let me illustrate: I have a strong opinion about the central theme of Scripture. However, I recognize others have different opinions. Rather than debate the issue, I will listen to their conclusion and ask how they came to it. I will offer my conclusion and how I came to it.

Some think the Bible is a random collection of myth, poetry, history, and moral teachings. Some see it chiefly as a user's manual—a moral guide for human beings. Some see it as a book of prophecy to be used to figure out what is going to happen next. Some see it as a book that shows God's sovereign rule over all nature and all people. Some see it as the message of God's salvation through the death and resurrection of Christ. Some say all of the above. In fact, all of the issues listed—and many others—can be found in Scripture. But which one is your imperative? Which one has led you into a ministry that may have caused personal sacrifices and other difficulties? Which one would make you get out of bed at 2 A.M. to be with a dying person in the hospital? Which one makes you want to preach next Sunday?

My imperative comes from two places.

In 1 Corinthians 15, Paul wrote, "If that is true, it means that Christ was not raised; and if Christ has not been raised from death, then we have nothing to preach and you have nothing to believe" (verses 13–14).

Next, right before he ascended into heaven, Jesus told his believers to go to the world and teach everything he had commanded. I am a believer; therefore, I am to teach what Jesus taught. I once read a book by a historian who gave a report on Jesus from his professional point of view. He said the apostle Paul was amazingly ignorant of the teachings of Jesus. Of course that got my attention, but I figured out what he meant. Paul didn't make a big deal about retelling Jesus' parables or retelling the great miracles. He didn't quote Jesus from the Sermon on the Mount in Matthew or the High Priestly Prayer from John's gospel. Paul does put an emphasis on two doctrines from Jesus' curriculum—Baptism and the Lord's Supper.

This does not mean that Paul was unaware of the teachings of Jesus. Rather, it shows he understood Jesus' mission. The Messiah's job description included healing the sick and proclaiming Good News for all people. But his primary task was to make the Good News true by doing battle against the two enemies of all people—sin and death. Paul knew that to teach what Christ commanded was to do more than teach his words. The apostle's big message was always the death and resurrection of Christ for our salvation.

Jesus' introductory line to the great commission is, "I have been given all authority in heaven and on earth" (Matthew 28:18). He had come to earth as the Son of God who therefore had authority over all that God had created. Then as he is ready to depart, he claims all authority—even over what God had not created, that is sin and death.

We who believe are sent to the world with the message of Christ's redemption of all people. Put that in your sermon and preach it!

CHAPTER 2

Why Use Illustrations?

A wannabe book illustrator once came to me with a long series of completed pictures for a children's book. He wanted me to write a story for the illustrations. Because I like a novel idea now and then, I tried it. No go! I had to explain that illustrations were made for stories, not stories for illustrations.

My effort to write a story to fit the pictures was not wasted. The lesson I learned applies to our present project. Sermons are not made for illustrations; illustrations are made for sermons. However, it is important to note that they are not a quick fix for a flat sermon, nor are they meant for comic or other varieties of relief for listeners who are suffering through a sermon.

I have approached writing this book with the same struggles I felt when I prepared most of my sermons. I am aware, and hope you are too, of how easily it is for listeners and readers to misunderstand and misuse a message. The anxiety I feel does not make me avoid preaching or writing sermons. Rather, it makes me aware of the importance of hard work in preparing and delivering a sermon. I must work on this book for your reading, not for my writing. You must prepare your sermons for the members of your congregation's hearing, not for your speaking. Do not preach defensively—that is to protect yourself from being misunderstood. Instead, preach offensively—that is, to help your hearers understand. I am trying to follow my own advice as I write this.

Let me illustrate: I started my ministry in Southern Mississippi in the early 1960s. I was in a small town with no members of my denomination and the nearest sister congregation was 70 miles away. Do I have to explain I got lonely? I tried to find other Christian clergy I could relate to. To my horror, I found most of them were members of the KKK and proud of it. They openly preached that God required racial segregation.

Then I found one minister who knew racism was wrong. We could talk to each other about Christ and how the Gospel applied to the racial struggles. Both of us saw that the way to change was not through violence, but through the love of Christ. Since those who joined my church knew my denomination's position on race, we had only a few members, but they were with me. He had a larger congregation. I asked him how he could preach what he believed without getting into trouble. He answered, "I say it often, but I talk about it in ways the people don't understand." I lost a friend that day, but I learned a lesson in the sacredness of preaching. We are doing a holy thing when we teach the word of God. We dare not play word or theological games. We must use every resource available to give a clear message from God.

Illustrations can make or break a sermon. They are so important that we who preach can be tempted to use them as insurance for keeping our audience awake. Because people respond to our illustrations, we can use them as a short cut to a sermon that gets attention. But I do not like hearing a sermon when it is obvious the illustrations came from some book of sermon aids and the preacher's chief work on the sermons was searching for illustrations rather than searching the Scripture. In my opinion, books of sermon illustrations do for homiletics what fast food does for cuisine. This book will include many illustrations that I hope you can adapt to your need and use, but its primary purpose is to help you make better use of the illustrations others and I offer you—and, more importantly, to help you find and create your own.

Just as your sermon must have a purpose, so also each illustration in the sermon must have a purpose that helps attain the goal of the sermon. Let's think about some reasons why illustrations help make a sermon effective.

ILLUSTRATIONS SHINE LIGHT ON A SUBJECT

The primary value of illustrations comes from the word itself—an illustration illuminates a subject. Let me illustrate:

You are leading your congregation on a nature trail at night. Your job is to know the trail so you can lead others and help them learn the trail. As you lead them down the path, you tell them a tree to their right is an important landmark. It has a broken limb about 12 feet up the trunk. They need to recognize that tree so they can follow the trail on their own. The hikers see the tree but can't see the distinguishing mark. You turn your flashing light on and point it to the broken limb in the tree. All of the hikers say, "I see it."

When you preach, you are leading your congregation through God's word. They need to learn the way through the word so they can follow the trail. You explain a marker in Scripture that is important for understanding the message. It may be a sign that shows them their sin. It may be one that shows them salvation through Jesus Christ. But the way is dark. They don't recognize the sign. So you use an illustration to shine light on the sign. They see the message through the light of the illustration. They say, "I get it." But notice that the illustration is not the mark on the trail that they need to learn; the illustration illuminates the mark so they can see it and learn the way.

Let's make a few more applications of the flashlight illustration.

The beam of a flashlight doesn't reveal anything until it is directed toward something that reflects the light back to the viewers. You can't follow a beam from a flashlight that points into space.

The person using the flashlight must know the way. Illustrations are not searchlights randomly seeking to locate something to look at. The light must focus on one subject so both speaker and hearers are getting the same message.

The light must point to something that is a part of the text being applied to the hearers. You may find other interesting things to look at through an illustration, but illustrations can make people loose the trail if they have nothing to do with the message.

The purpose of a flashlight is to point to something other than itself. Those who follow you on the hike get the wrong message if they go home and say, "Our leader had a great flashlight."

When the flashlight is turned off, the people still remember what they saw.

Sermons need illustrations because we who preach must deal with profound and complex ideas. We use words in special ways. When one of us says, "I hope you get well," our sentence has a different meaning than Paul's when he talks about our hope in Christ. Our definitions of words such as guilt, repent, faith, forgiveness, love, and others all have special meanings because we use them with the Christian trademark. Yet people are used to hearing these words with generic meanings. We often need an illustration to show we have something special in mind by those words.

We also frequently use concepts which are not a part of the everyday conversations of our hearers. We can talk about original sin, justification by faith, body of Christ, baptismal regeneration, vicarious atonement, and a long list of other theologically profound and spiritually necessary concepts. People may know the meaning of most of the words, but the combination of the words need illustration. (I once used the term *original sin* and someone asked, "Does that mean you have created a sin that only you have?" I claim a degree of creativity, but I'm not that good—or bad from another point of view.)

Your assignment: Look for ideas that need illumination. Then look for a good illustration that will help those who hear your sermon say, "I see." Do not look for good illustrations to throw in a sermon now and then.

ILLUSTRATIONS DO NOT PROVE A POINT

Illustrations help us understand something, but they do not prove something. A pastor who was an amateur magician often used magic effectively in children's sermons. Once he had a liquid that would boil at slightly below body temperature. He put the liquid in a test tube and carefully held the glass by the edge. He told the children, "This is a test to see if Jesus loves you. If you hold the test tube and the liquid boils, it will mean that Jesus loves you." The first child took the glass in her hand and the liquid soon boiled. The same thing happened with the next child, and the next. They were amazed because the liquid would boil as soon as another child held it. Until one child, who apparently had extremely cold hands, took the test tube. No matter how long she held it, the liquid would not boil. This shows the danger of a good illustration gone awry. It was a hands-on experience; that is good. It used the senses; that is good. But the proof that Jesus loves us comes from a cross, not a test tube.

I planned to use the flash on a camera in a sermon. You guessed it: though I followed my own rules and checked everything before the service started, the flash did not work. I changed the purpose of my illustrating by saying, "This shows you can't trust anything but Jesus." There is a rule somewhere (maybe I just made it up) that says, "The better the illustration the more likely something can go wrong." Don't let that keep you from finding, creating, and using good illustrations. However, remember that they do not prove your point. They illuminate it.

ILLUSTRATIONS PROVIDE POINTS-OF-MEMORY

As you remember past sermons, both those you have preached and those you have heard, chances are you will first remember an illustration. The illustration will provide a point-of-memory (if it was connected to the text and to the sermon) that will help you recall other parts of the sermon.

I'd like to leave a blank page here as a place for you to fill in your memories about sermons. Instead, I'll suggest you take a breather from reading and see how far back you can remember a sermon. Then I'll tell you about a sermon I remember.

Before I became a pastor, I heard a sermon with the following illustration. A man was in financial problems and decided to sell a ring his deceased mother had received from a member of the royal family of England. His mother had worked for that family, and the ring was a gift from them when she left. It was always displayed as the family treasure. The man could not believe it when the jeweler told him the stone was fake and the gold of poor quality. "But it came from royalty," he protested. "Even royalty sometimes give cheap gifts," the jeweler replied.

With the story in mind, I tried to recall the sermon. It was preached during Advent. The pastor applied his story, "Royalty may give a cheap gift, but God never does. He sent his own Son to be our Savior."

You will notice many of the illustrations I repeat in this book are connected with points-of-memory. If you remember one point, it starts a chain that connects you to other points from the past. I suggest you do this when you need something to keep your mind occupied. When you recall points-of-memory from your own past, you will remember some good illustrations, and you will also learn how to put points-of-memory into your future sermons. As you recall previous sermons, you may learn from negative experiences as well as positive ones.

POINTS-OF-MEMORY FOR THE PREACHER

Using illustrations as points-of-memory can be helpful both to the preacher and to the congregation. First, let's consider ourselves.

I noticed something first in others who preach, then realized it's true of me as well. We are more relaxed during the parts of a sermon when we are telling a story or using an object lesson. As I listened to others use illustrations, I noticed their voices became more natural, they were freed from their manuscripts or notes, and their language used more everyday words. After I saw this in others, I watched for the same experience in myself. It was there.

Think about it. As you present the message of your sermon, you are thinking about the order of the message. With or without a manuscript, you are keeping part of your mind on what is coming next. Then when you have a story to tell, you relax; you just tell the story. We do it all the time. As you become more comfortable, so do those who hear you.

Two applications for you: Plan your illustrations to give yourself a break in the sermon. If you need one, the congration does also. If each illustration is connected to the text and to your plan for the sermon, the points-of-memory will not take your mind and the minds of those who hear you away from the main message. Instead, they will help you keep your sermon organized for your own presentation.

Second: Learn the rest of your sermon in blocks and teach them with a point-of-memory. Though each segment may not have an illustration, the same idea may apply. Learn to present the text to the congregation as you would a story. Do the same with the explanation of a doctrine or an application.

Points-of-Memory for the Hearers

When illustrations are a part of the integrity of a sermon, they not only provide an "I see" in the minds of the listeners during the worship service, they also provide a point-of-memory for continued use of the sermon. When those who heard the sermon draw an illustration you used up on their memory screen, the rest of the sermon will be recalled too—at least a good part of it.

I like to look at it this way. Notice the number of people in church who have family members who are not there—sometimes never there. Those people who are in church have contact with many other people during the week. Suppose one of those nonattending family members or a co-worker asks, "What was the sermon about?" I doubt if many of those who heard the sermon will quote the text or the title of the sermon from the bulletin (though a few may, and may their numbers increase). More likely, the one who went to church will answer by giving an illustration from the sermon. From that point-of-memory, a discussion might follow that includes other details of the sermon. Let me illustrate:

You go to a restaurant for a meal and are served more food than you can eat at that time. You ask for a doggy bag, and take the extra food home. Later you may eat the leftovers yourself, or you could share them with someone else. The point is, the restaurant not only provided the abundance of food, but also gave you the container to take the leftovers home.

Your sermon offers spiritual food. The menu of Scripture offers so much that no one can consume all that is served. So as you prepare the meal with its abundance, also plan a doggy bag for those who worship. Give them something to use to take home the message for their own use during the week, or so they can give the extra to someone else.

Illustrations of all kinds, stories, object lessons, concepts (a later chapter is on this subject) make excellent containers for those who hear a sermon to take the message home. They serve the dual purpose of helping the hearer receive the message and helping those who worship do their own ministry by sharing the message with others.

Illustrations as Points-of-Contact

Every worship service needs to build a two-way bridge that crosses a wide canyon. One side of the canyon is the world in which we live. It is a world of sinners living among sinners. It is where might makes right. Those who have the power create the justice. People are insecure at their jobs, with their family relationships, about their health, and about their future. It is a place with many wonderful things and beautiful experiences, but each of the good things makes people aware that the good might not last. Worst of all, the world is filled with walls that divide us and subdivide us until, at times, each person is alone.

On the other side of the canyon is the presence of God. There we are loved because of who God is, rather than who we are. There we live not by justice, but by the grace that God gave us through Jesus Christ when he came over the bridge to our side, defeated the power of sin and death, and went back across the bridge. There is no condemnation, no competition, and no fear on that side of the bridge. There are no walls to divide us.

When I first became a pastor, I used to write prayers in the bulletin for people to use as they prepared for worship. Most of them went something like this:

> Dear God, help me to forget all the problems and disappointments in the world so I may worship you with true joy and devotion through Jesus Christ, our Lord and Savior. Amen.

I wanted the worship service to be a time-out from the struggles of life—and I had it half right. I still pray that the worship I do, and the worship I lead, brings others and me before the glorious throne of God. I still want to see the glory of God so clearly that I forget everything else. But now my prayers are different. They are more like this:

> Lord Jesus, I bring my guilt, pains, and sorrow with me and place them at your throne of grace. Bless me and others who worship here so we may go back to our lives renewed by our love and mercy. Amen.

I do not want my worship, or the worship I lead, to deny the reality of daily life. I want to confront the depth of guilt with the height of grace. I want to expose all fear to the light of God's protection in Jesus Christ. I want no temporary truce between the evil of my own life and the grace of my new life in Jesus Christ; I want the battle to be fought because I know who wins.

It's easy for those of us who plan and lead worship services to stay on one side of the bridge. We can become so excited about worship and the message of God's word that we forget people who have little or no awareness of proper worship and true doctrine. We can become so otherworldly that we're no earthly good.

Or, we can become so concerned about our problems and the problems of people in our congregation and community that we forget that God has dealt with the problems through Jesus Christ. We can identify so much with the needs of people that we forget to show them what Christ has done for them. We can jump into a drowning world to save them—and drown with them.

Reality check: Which side of the bridge do you spend more time on? Is your foot planted more firmly on the heaven side? Or the earth side? From which side of the bridge do you preach your sermons? Would the members of your congregation agree with your self-assessment?

Illustrations are *one* way to walk both directions across the bridge that connects the presence of God and the presence of people. In this case the idea of an illustration also becomes an illustration. As I talk about using illustrations that have a point-of-contact in the presence of God and also a point-of-contact in our world, I will be concerned about the job description of this book. However since I am promoting the use of illustrations, I hope you can see how these points-of-contact on both sides of the canyon apply not only to sermon illustrations, but also to music, liturgy, Scripture readings, and other parts of the worship service.

Remember that your sermon must introduce your two friends, the text and the members of the congregation, to each other so they find something to talk about. Each illustration helps find those points-of-contact. An illustration can start in the word (on God's side of the canyon) and lead across the bridge to our side. Or the illustration can make a point-of-contact with us on our side and lead us across the bridge to make a point-of-contact with God.

Let me illustrate from 2 Samuel 12: Nathan came to see King David. He told a story about a rich man who used his power to take advantage of a poor man. The king in David's time was the head of all three powers of government: the executive, the legislative, and the judicial. He made the law, he was the chief law officer, and he was the judge in every case. The story that Nathan told required action. Such an injustice must be punished, and King David would see that justice was administered. Then the prophet Nathan took David across the bridge into the presence of God. "You are the man," Nathan said and explained his illustration.

When David listened to Nathan's story, he said, "I see." But he had only seen one point-of-contact. When he saw the second point-of-contact, he was in the presence of God. David said, "I have sinned against the LORD."

Or, the first point-of-contact can be on God's side of the canyon. Tell your version of John's vision in Revelation 4. Describe the scene. Hear the music. Then cross the bridge to the human side of the canyon with two sentences, "Jesus said he was going to prepare a place for you. There it is."

Jesus started many of his parables by saying, "The kingdom of God is like. ..." That was from his Father's side of the bridge. Then he would tell stories from our side—about farmers and fisherman, about families, about baking bread and cleaning the house. Those who heard—and those who hear—his stories are on the human side of the canyon, but by his illustrations he shows us God is with us on our side. When we realize that God is among us, we can look for the bridge that brought him to us and will take us to him.

We do not have to establish the points-of-contact. God has done that. He has built the bridge. Look at the way God works both sides of the canyon:

Jesus is God. God the Father goes to the witness stand three times and identifies Jesus in the human lineup by saying, "This is my Son." Yet Jesus becomes a human—a resident on our side of the canyon. He has a family, is a citizen, and works a job. The only human trait he didn't have was sin and its successor death, but he took the responsibility for ours. When you preach Christ, you can make the point-of-contact on either side. You can tell of God who crossed the bridge to become one of us. You can tell about the man who destroyed the power of sin and death and crossed the bridge back to God with a message, "You all come, you hear!"

The Scripture is God's Word. Through it, God speaks with authority. Through it, the Holy Spirit leads us to repentance and to faith. It is a point-of-contact on God's side of the canyon. But people who are like us wrote the Bible on this side. It is for people, and it is about people, dealing with all the range of human experience. The Bible itself offers "I see" moments as we read it to discover what God does when he encounters people and what he says when he talks to us.

We receive the Lord's Supper as guests of Jesus Christ. In that meal, we receive his body and His blood. The meal takes us across the canyon to receive something beyond our scientific and logical experiences. It gives us a point-of-contact in Christ. However, it also has a point-of-contact in our everyday world. In that banquet from heaven we also eat bread and drink wine. The same Scripture that tells us it is the body and blood of Christ also speaks of it as the cup and the loaf. I like it when I can taste the fruit in the wine and the wheat in the bread; that's part of the real human presence. When we eat the meal, we are on both sides of the canyon.

From the lofty heights of the person of Jesus Christ, the inspiration of Scripture, and the sacredness of the Sacrament of the Altar, we come to the illustrations in your sermons. I am not comparing our human efforts to the great acts of God.

But our message is a continuation of the proclamation of God who crossed the canyon and came to us in Jesus Christ. We know God not because we went to him, but because he came to us. His point-of-contact with us happened on our side of the bridge. By faith we have followed him to his side.

The illustrations in your sermons give you an excellent opportunity to identify both points-of-contact in your life. You can start with the glory of God and lead to the reality of human life. You can start in the mire of hopelessness and lead to the presence of God in heaven. You can start with the mind and logic and lead to faith and grace. Or, you can start with spiritual power of God and lead to the human weakness of sins.

Illustrations are an opportunity to connect. You connect one end of the illustration to the Scripture and the other end to the people who hear your message.

CHAPTER 3

Sermon X Rays

We now turn our attention to the sermons you have preached and those you have heard. We're going to x-ray those sermons to see the structure rather than the message.

For two chapters I have emphasized that the function of a sermon—the message it delivers—is of highest importance. Now we turn to the form of the sermon to see that good planning helps deliver a good message.

To x-ray a sermon, turn your attention away from the content and listen to the method used to communicate the message. Later I will show you some x rays of typical sermon patterns. First I want to tell you how I learned to x-ray sermons and teach you to do the same.

Long ago, I realized I do not learn much about communication from good speakers. They are good (from my point of view) because they present a clear message I understand. They communicate with such ease that I don't notice their methods. The attention is on the message, and I learn what they have to teach. All they do for me is remind me I want the same results when I preach.

I have learned even less about communication from the great speakers I have heard. They are so good that often their powers of communication outshine the message they have to deliver. While I am awed by them, I learn little because I know I can't preach that way and I'd make a fool of myself if I tried. They have special talents from God, education, and experiences that are out of my range. I enjoy hearing them— but as my heroes, not my teachers.

My primary communication teachers have been poor speakers because they have taught me to x-ray sermons—and other speeches. Long ago, I ignored poor speakers. Within a sentence or two it is easy to tell if a speaker has anything to say and any idea about how to say it. If I got a negative on both of those issues, I tuned to my own thoughts. I decided I wouldn't let them waste my time. But I learned better.

When I was new in the preaching game, I rode to a clergy conference with an older pastor. On the way, he told me who would preach at the opening worship. He also told me that if I watched the guy preach, I would get nothing out of the sermon because he always looked at the church rafters while he talked. "But," the older pastor told me, "this man has something worthwhile to say. Don't look at him. Just listen."

The advice was correct. I got a lot out of the sermon that day because I avoided looking at the pastor and at the church rafters. But I learned something else. Listening to a sermon is not a passive experience. Who am I to sit there and think that the speaker has to pour the message in me? I learned to work at listening.

My first problem: I didn't get to hear many speakers. In the seminary we had a big supply of speakers, and my job was to listen. Then, in the moment of a laying-on-of-hands ceremony, the roles reversed. I did the talking, and others listened. First solution: I joined a civic club and listened to a speaker every week. You might get some help by listening to speakers on TV and radio, but their methods must be different, and many are working with writers, editors, and coaches you don't have on your staff. Besides, they are talking to strangers; you are talking to people you know and who know you. Listen to real speakers at weddings, funerals, official functions of employers, schools, civic affairs, etc. Don't stay away because it will be boring: That's the reason to go. You'll learn how not to be boring. Above all, don't tune them out because you disagree with them. You learn when you listen to someone who has a different view than you. Of course, you might learn you could possibly be wrong on something. But more than that, you learn how to present an opposing view without driving the audience away.

Listen as though you are x-raying the sermon. Listen beyond the words and hear what the speaker is trying to say. Use your experience and knowledge to supplement those of the speaker. Then you will get an x-ray view of the sermon.

X RAYS OF THE BODY OF A SERMON

First lets adjust our x-ray ears to view the sermon as a whole. We want to see the framework of the sermon.

Theme and Parts.

The first x ray looks like this:

Figure 1.

This is a view of a classical way to present a message. The first line is an introduction. The second (centered) is the theme of the message. The following series of lines followed by indented lines are the parts. The final line is the conclusion. This is an excellent way to present information because it uses linear thinking.

This theme-and-part format is the most common for sermon structuring and can serve like a basic black dress for a woman's wardrobe. It's always something that you can rely on, and by using a variety of accessories you can make it fit many different occasions. Let me illustrate a simple theme and part sermon. The text is James 2:14–17.

Theme: I believe; therefore I do.

1. What do you believe?

2. What do you do about it?

Look at any text and find the message of faith. The same outline then becomes:

Theme: Name the chief thought of the text.

For example:

God has revealed himself to us in Jesus Christ.

(Name any specific or category of sin) affects our lives.

(Name any way to serve God) affects our lives.

(Name any doctrine of Scripture) affects our lives.

1. What do you believe about it?

2. What do you do about it?

The theme/part method of preaching is versatile; however, it has some downsides.

1. This form of communication is better for the written page than the spoken word. On a page (as I am doing right now) the writer can outline thoughts, and the reader can glance back to review the order of the thought. A hearer does not have that opportunity. The idea of linear thinking came with the printing press and made a great contribution to our ability to record and transmit ideas.

Linear thinkers, who have done most of their learning by reading and hearing, find this the best way to both receive and transmit information. However, the coming of TV has decreased the number of linear thinkers—even among educated people. Even those who make their living at linear-thinking jobs during the week often appreciate a break on weekends.

2. The theme/part method has been helpful to many speakers because it provides a memory pattern for them as they speak. Each of the parts may begin with a word that starts with the same letter of the alphabet. For this book on illustrations, I could have the following parts: Images, Ideas, and Icons. Notice how I stretched to get the last one. A danger arises in changing the message to fit the structure. Remember, the message picks the structure—not the other way around. Or, the parts can have words that fit together. For a sermon from Acts 2 at the end of Pentecost, the parts could be Fellowship, Stewardship, and Churchmanship. In both of the above examples, the way to remember the parts helps the speaker more than the hearers. Rarely do the three-part series of words come from the biblical text so people will remember them when they read the text again. They may help only in short-term memory—that is, until the next sermon is preached. The ideas must relate to the hearers in order to become a part of long-term memory.

3. The theme/part method requires high listening skills in the hearers. No one can concentrate on one idea for over a few minutes—and that may be stretching it. When readers lose the train of thought, they can go back a few paragraphs and start over. When listeners take a little mental side trip, they have no way of catching up to the speaker's line of thought. In theme/part sermons, like algebra class, once you miss a block of the message, you might as well give up.

4. I think every preacher should use the theme/part method some time. However, when used every week, the preparation process can reverse so the message is adjusted to fit the formula—rather than the message looking for an appropriate method. One pastor told me it took him over 20 years to stop preaching every sermon with the outline Goal, Malady, Means. That outline can be a great way to proclaim some texts to some congregations. However, when sermon study starts with a preconceived outline, the message is taken from its natural habitat and put in a cage.

Many speakers use the theme/parts method very effectively. They start by showing you an x-ray view of the message, then lead you through it by referring to the parts of the outline. Listen to other speakers and watch for their theme and parts. Does the structure help present the message? Or, does it conceal the message? Was the message adjusted to fit the structure? Or, was the structure chosen to reveal the message?

Now try the same examination on your own sermons. Remember, your sermon is for your congregation—not for an editor, professor, or other readers.

String of Pearls (Beads)

Another disadvantage to the theme/parts structure of a sermon is the system often transmutes into what is kindly called a string of pearls. The speaker transmits theme and parts, but the hearers receive a string of beads (Figure 2).

The speaker starts with an idea, and the hearers go along from idea to idea. In the ideal situation the string has a clasp on each end, and the journey ends up back where it started with the beginning and the end at the same place. In reality, the trip is often one-way.

I think I have learned about communication (but not about the subject at hand) from listening to those who use this method more than any other. There is a reason: To fol-

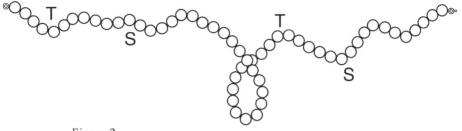

Figure 2

low such a speaker from bead to bead in search of a pearl, one must listen intensely.

The best news is that for those who listen, there are pearls among the beads. In our sound-byte generation many people like to be able to tune in and out at will. As much as the communicator in me wants to condemn this method, I have to admit that for some people it works. A story here, a quote there, a Bible verse once in a while— somebody will get something out of the message. However, what they get may not be what the speaker intended to deliver.

I heard a funeral sermon by a pastor I admired but had never heard speak before. I had been told he rambled, so I went with my sermon x-ray machine and a determination to follow him. The sermon started with his recent trip to Scotland and then went to the wool items he had bought. From there, we went to sheep—and suddenly I was ahead of him. Sheep would lead to dogs. The deceased had nine dogs. The dogs would lead back to sheep. The sheep would lead us to Psalm 23. It worked for me. I assume others who knew both the pastor and the dearly departed were able to follow the message. But I'm afraid the rest were left somewhere in Scotland.

You may think I am suggesting this method as a way to force your hearers to pay attention. Wrong! I am suggesting you listen intently to this method so you can be kinder to your parishioners. I don't think you should do all the work for your listeners, but I do think there are better ways to get them involved in the message. We'll work on that later.

In some situations, the string-of-beads/pearls method works well. For example, some texts are just waiting to be understood. You pick up one end of the text as though it were a string. You ask everyone to be with you at that place, and you follow the string through the text and let the pearls fall in their laps. Don't do this every Sunday, but it might be a good idea after you've done a series of highly organized, linear-thinking, theme/part sermons. The reverse is also true. If you have been pearl diving for several weeks, go back to Goal, Malady, Means and give a good linear-thinking sermon.

String of Pearls without the String

There can be yet another transmutation. The poorly prepared sermon becomes beads and/or pearls without a string. The x ray shows it this way:

Figure 3

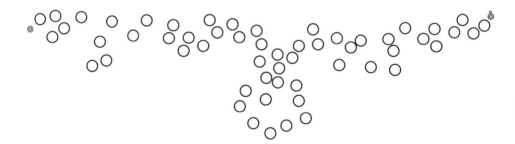

From the speakers' point of view this is still a string of pearls. But too often the string exists only in the minds of those who speak. It comes from their experiences, their reading material, and their interests. The speakers may have reasons to jump from one subject to another, but the hearers don't know those reasons. When I hear these kinds of sermons, I have this visual of the preacher throwing the beads out in the congregation and all of us scrambling under the pews trying to find something for us. It doesn't work for me.

In some worship services, it is obvious more attention was paid to having a unified worship service and a unified message. The hymns, prayers, lessons go together. I appreciate that—and that work should help give a unified message to the sermon also.

Because I'm an optimist about the intentions of Christian pastors, and because I believe the Holy Spirit works through the word of Scripture, I admit some good can come from these disconnected sermons. All of us have done it once in a while—at least in the minds of some hearers. God forgives us. The congregation does to. But in behalf of your congregation I add, "Go, and ramble no more!"

TIME OUT FOR THINKING ADJUSTMENT

We have more x rays of sermons, but they are in a different category. The first three showed linear thinking from the best to the worst; now we will switch to conceptual thinking. In the reality of both writing and speaking many shades of both methods exist. Comparing the two is not an issue of good or bad, right or wrong; it is a difference in methods.

Conceptual thinking starts with an idea that is defined then expanded. At first it may seem some conceptions are illustrations—there's a chapter about that later. But the concept is more than an illustration.

Take, for example, this chapter. It is called "Sermon X rays." The idea of x-raying a sermon is not just an illustration to start the chapter; it is a concept used throughout the chapter. I explained the idea of x-raying a sermon, then showed a variety of ways of doing it. There is a little bit of linear thinking in the way I am listing the different examples, but not much. Each idea directly connects to the concept; thus, they could be used in a different order. If this works as well as I hope it does, you will understand the concept and add your own examples.

Psalm 23 is an excellent example of conceptual thinking. The basic concept is "The Lord is my Shepherd." From then on the existing verses could be used in random order— although it's good to end with David's last line. People paraphrase and add to the concept of the Good Shepherd—even way beyond church property lines.

Or, consider 1 Corinthians 13. The concept is delivered in the last line of the previous chapter. From then on Paul keeps coming back to the better definition of love as he shares a variety of ideas. We can use part or all of them, bringing in other ideas about love as well. Now let's look at some x rays of conceptual sermons.

The Bicycle Wheel

The concept is the hub—the core of the message. All ideas are related to that hub. It looks this way on an x ray:

Figure 4

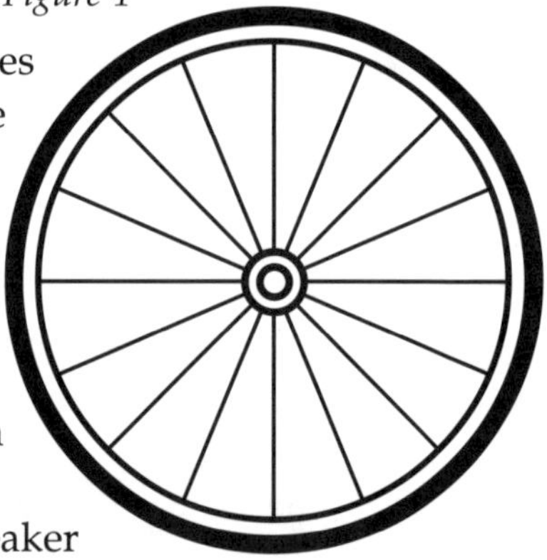

Notice each idea relates directly to the concept of the sermon. In theme/part sermons, it is easy for the parts to become children and grandchildren of the theme. In the string-of-whatever sermons, follow-up ideas can become stepchildren.

This method is both speaker and hearer-friendly. The speaker needs to define the concept both clearly and briefly, then develop each idea from that concept. If the hearers understand the concept, they can miss one or more of the spokes of the wheel and still get a good part of the message. They can also add their own spokes to the wheel and give the preacher the credit.

Let me illustrate:

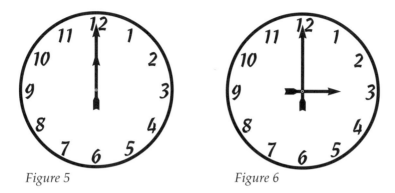

Figure 5   Figure 6

The text is Galatians 4:4–7. The visual image is a clock face with moveable hands. You may describe the concept without using the visual. If you do, refer to your watch and ask the hearers to do the same. (Digital watches will mess you up.)

CONCEPT: Check the Time.

Put the small hand behind the large one on the first clock face. Explain we cannot tell the time with only one hand. Is this the large hand or the small one? Then place the large hand at 12 and move the small hand to several numbers to show the time.

Today's text tells us God did something special at the right time. We want to check his time. Use the second clock face with the small hand behind the large one. Point the two hands briefly to each of the four items on the clock face. We could talk about each of these subjects as separate issues. But the point of the text is that, on schedule, Christ came to the world to give us a different view of each of these subjects. We're going to put the big hand on Christ. Then put the small one on each of the subjects to see it in a special way because Christ has come.

1. At the right time Christ was born of a human mother. (Big hand on Christ, small hand on Human.) "I'm only human" used to be an excuse for failure, limitations, and even sin. Use your study of the text to talk about what it means that Christ was born of a human mother. We call

him the only-begotten Son of God. Begotten could be misunderstood; it is an old word that we don't use too much outside of church. Begotten is the past tense of beget. A mother conceives and gives birth; a father begets, meaning that he causes the mother to conceive and give birth. Therefore, we are all begotten. The difference between Jesus and us is that our life started when our Father begot and our mother conceived us. Christ is the only Son who existed from eternity, begotten of God the Father "before all worlds" (Nicene Creed). Then in time, Mary conceived by the power of the Holy Spirit, on schedule by God's plan. Today Christ is still the Son of Mary as well as Son of God. He is still human as well as divine. When he rose again he was exalted in his human nature as well as his divinity. He remains God with us as we celebrate at his birth, and also human as the Son of Mary. Explain the importance of seeing the humanity of Christ in order to understand our Savior's work for us and in our place.

2. Back to the clock. At the right time, Jesus was born under the Law. Show it on the clock face. We can talk about the Law of God by itself, but it is different when one hand points to the Law and the other points to Christ. He came under the Law to keep it for us. Explain how our use of the Law is different because Christ is with us under the Law. Include the fact that we don't have to defend ourselves or accuse others. Christ has removed the cure of the Law by his death for us.

3. Back to the clock. We can talk about God without Christ; many people do. But in Christ we see God in a different way. The Spirit of Christ in us makes us call God "Father." Use your study of the text to show how we live in a different relationship with God because his Son is our brother. We are no longer slaves, but we are children of God.

CONCLUSION: The right time for Christ to come to the world was not just the day of his birth. We don't know what day, month, or year that he was born, but we know he came to earth for all time. Today we see our lives in a different way because Christ is with us.

End of illustration. (For further use of this illustration see chapter 11, page 227.)

Notice that the concept used in the introduction also introduces each part of the sermon. By starting again at the same place (the hub of the wheel) for each section you help yourself and your hears remember the purpose of your sermon and to identify each of the thoughts about it.

The Daisy

The previous concept going one step farther can be seen in the next x ray:

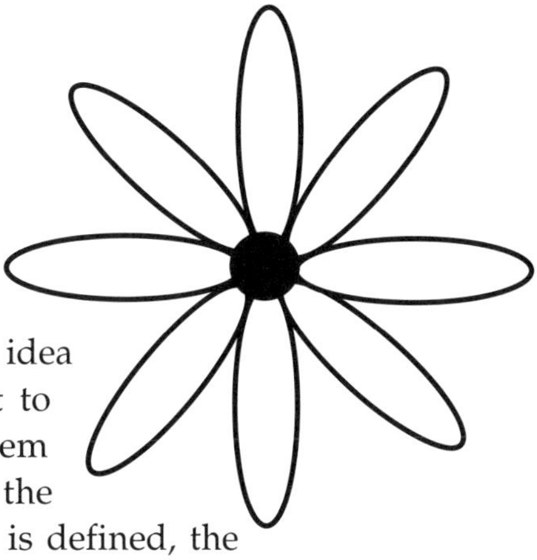

Figure 7

The outline of a daisy is an upgrade of the bicycle wheel model, because each idea starts at the center, goes out to the hearers, and brings them back to the center. The eye of the daisy is the concept. Once it is defined, the speaker and the congregation can make as many trips out and back as necessary. If those who listen skip a few of the trips, they haven't lost the entire message. Some of them may even make a few side excursions on their own and make their own applications from the concept.

The bicycle wheel and daisy methods both make a sermon more adaptable for different uses. You may develop a good concept for a wedding or funeral sermon. With that concept as the eye of your daisy you can preach a number of different sermons by using more, less, or different petals. I had a number of conceptual sermons that I would use repeatedly for weddings and funerals by changing the pedals. One member of the congregation, a pastor's widow, would always catch me, but she took great delight in our little game, so it worked well.

Also, if you have a dual parish or have multiple services in one congregation, the daisy method helps adjust the same sermon for different worship services. For the last 16 years of my ministry, I preached each sermon four times—from Saturday night to Sunday noon. Each of the services developed a different personality. Those who go to an 8 A.M. service are more serious. Those who go on Saturday night have already shown a disregard for tradition. The same sermon could easily be adjusted for each service.

Because of the number of services, we had to keep on schedule. This can be difficult when both the school music teacher and the choir director decide to hit the heights of musical ecstasy, all three lessons are long, and the Stephen Ministry director wants to honor all past classes as a way to promote the new class that starts Tuesday night—all in the same service. Dropping a pedal or two off the daisy can shorten the sermon. I have done this many times, and often (not always) I have felt the shorter sermon was more effective.

The next chapter has a number of illustrations using the daisy as a model. Let's use an illustration here to give you the picture. The text is Isaiah 35. The title is: Travel on the Holy Road.

CONCEPT: Isaiah tells us that God has built a road to rescue us, called the Holy Road. In Isaiah's time roads were not designed by engineers or built by construction companies. First, animals made a path. Then both other animals and humans who hunted the animals followed that same path. Soon the path became a lane, and then the lane became a road. The road was made because it was used. God made a path to us when he came to us through the messages delivered by prophets. They prepared the way that became a Holy Road when Christ followed that path and came to be our Savior. Use material from verses 8–10 to describe that road.

1. Sinners were not allowed on the Holy Road. If deer make a path, it is a deer path. If hunters use that path to kill the

deer, it becomes a hunters' lane. God made a Holy Road. If sinners traveled the road, it would become a sinners' road. But Christ paid the toll so we could travel on his Holy Road. By his death for our sins, he removed our guilt. Christ stands at the entrance to the Holy Road. When we travel through him, we travel under his grace and forgiveness.

2. Christ is at the entrance ramp of the Holy Road, but because we are sinners we also make exits from the road. We go our way rather than Christ's way. We follow the paths that other sinners have made. We make new paths into the desert of sin and others follow us.

3. Below are a list of possible exits from the Holy Road and the way Christ brings us back in each case. Use some of these (or add some of your own) to show both how we build roads away from God out into the desert of sin, and how Christ builds the road to the place of our need to rescue us. In each case start from the Holy Road, go out to the human problem, and come back to the Holy Road.

    a. Verses 3 and 4. When we travel our own way and in the way of other sinners, we become weak, afraid, and discouraged. We feel we are alone and confused. Identify ways that we divide ourselves from each other and become lost in the desert of life. But Christ builds the Holy Road to our place of loneliness. He brings us back and gives us rest. He takes away our fear and confusion.

    b. Verses 5 and 6a. We have problems that limit our lives. Some are obvious. People are blind, deaf, and lame. People have cancer, AIDS, heart problems. Some of us have problems that are not easily seen and cannot be diagnosed by medical people. These physical problems are a part of our human experience. They are not individual punishments put on individual sinners, but they are a part of the pain that we cause each other and ourselves as we live in the desert of sin. But Christ comes to our place of pain. He leads us back to his Holy Road. We may carry our physical illnesses back on that road, but the guilt that adds to the burden is gone.

c. Verses 6b and 7. Use this section to identify special areas of pain. Talk about divisions in families, insecurity at work, fear of violence, and other problems that we have made. God created a world to be like the Garden of Eden. We have made it into a slum. God sent Jesus to come to live in the slum. The road he traveled to save us must be made in the areas that we live.

CONCLUSION: Remember that the Holy Road has both entrance and exit ramps. Adam and Eve took an exit ramp and made their own path of sin. God came to them with a promise of help and invited them back to travel on the Holy Road. We follow the trail of sin that leads us from God. But God always builds the Holy Road to where we are to reclaim us. Use the description of heaven in verse 9 to describe where the Holy Road takes us.

Notice that in this sermon the applications all lead out from and back to the picture of the Holy Road. You could use a visual of a map with cloverleaflike roads leading out from and back to the Holy Road. You could make other applications to special needs in your congregation or community.

The Spiral

The bicycle wheel or daisy sermon model can transmute into a spiral. The x ray looks like this:

Figure 8

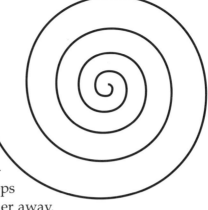

You may recognize this as a curled up version of a string of pearls. The speaker starts with a concept and goes out to the hearers, but never gets back. The preacher keeps circling the subject but keeps getting farther and farther away. The x ray will remind you of the path of a spaceship that ends up orbiting in outer space. Need I say more?

I will not give an illustration of the spiral as a model for a sermon because I don't want to suggest this method. Either of the illustrations given for the bicycle wheel or daisy model could degenerate to the spiral if the speaker did not go back to the concept to connect it with each new section.

Your Own X Rays

I don't suggest that the above six x rays cover every possible sermon structure. As you examine the sermons your preach and those you hear, you will recognize all of the above and perhaps find other models. The purpose of the sermon x ray is not to make you a faultfinder. It is to make you a good listener, in order to make you a better speaker. Look for the sermon structure that will best serve you as you deliver a message to your people. Also include some variety; it will help you pay more attention to your own sermons—and will help the congregation as well.

X Rays of Introductions

We now adjust our sermon x-ray machine to focus on introductions. The first few sentences of a sermon are critical. Those who listen are always willing to start with the speaker;

what they hear determines whether or not their minds will stay for the whole thing.

Comparing the x rays of the introductions of sermons with those of public addresses should show a big difference. Public speakers are taught that they need to give their audience an opportunity to know them before they get to their message. They tell a joke. They identify with the people before them by finding something they have in common. Several times I have seen speakers wearing a coat and tie. After they were introduced, they walk up front, take off their coat and tie, and say something like, "I feel comfortable with this group; so I think I'll relax."

None of that is needed for those who preach. The worship service itself bonds the preacher and the other worshipers, especially in liturgical churches. And it is true even if the one who preaches is not leading the rest of the worship service. The purpose of the introduction of a sermon is to introduce the people to the text and the text to the people— not to introduce the speaker.

In some sermons the introduction is too long. It is very discouraging to those who listen to hear the words "Now let's get to the text" when they thought they were close to "and in conclusion." Review the x rays shown earlier in this chaper. Now imagine that instead of the entire sermon, the x-ray was merely the introduction. Such lengthy beginnings are often a series of introductions, many of which have little to do with the planned message. Some of the items often included are the following:

1. Information about the source or relationship of the lessons of the day. Our job is to preach the text, not about the text. While we who preach should be well acquainted with the texts and the church year we follow, doing so is a part of our job. Once I turned on the car radio to a Christian station as I started a trip at 5 A.M. A preacher started his sermon by saying, "When you woke up this morning and first thought of the Propers of the Day," I thought he need-

ed a reality transfusion. When the sermon starts with those issues, we are asking the listeners to come into our world. A sermon should take the text to their world.

2. Details about events that happened in the congregation last week or (more often) those that will happen next week. In some cases they help the congregation understand the text. That's fine. In most cases they come off as commercials—and you know what we all do at home during commercials.

3. Stories that are intended to gain the attention of the congregation but have little or nothing to do with the sermon. Not a good idea. If you gain the attention of the listeners with a good story but have nothing to keep their interest, they will all notice that the sermon missed them. Of course, the alternative is not so good: If your sermon is dull, don't use a good introduction and no one will notice the dullness. Better method: Let your introduction and sermon be seen as one and the same—all applied to the listeners.

4. Comments about how well the choir sang, the good work of the altar guild, the weather that probably kept a lot of people away from church, and other chitchat that may not be necessary. If it is, it belongs someplace other than the beginning of sermon time.

Introductions to introductions confuse the serious listeners because they are not sure about the direction. Believe it or not, many people do check the text and the sermon title listed in the bulletin. They want to know what's going to happen. Tell them.

The minds of the less attentive listeners will be numbed by a long introduction and will wander in other directions. Remember the parishioners can also do their own version of a string of beads or a spiral sermon. A clear, concise introduction helps them start with you—and gives them a better chance to stay with you.

Finally, (don't get mad at me about this one) long introductions give the impression that the preacher is not well prepared and is waiting for inspiration to hit. You know that it takes more work to prepare a five-minute talk than a 45 minute one, if you have more time; you can keep talking until you hit the mark. For a short talk you cannot waste time.

Lengthy introductions are a bigger problem in conceptual sermons than those that follow linear thinking. In a theme/parts sermon you can at least get down to business after the long introduction and maybe the hearers will forget the distraction. In a conceptual sermon the clutter stays in the center and you will trip over it again and again.

X Rays of the Text in the Sermon

Again, we adjust our x-ray machine—this time to locate the text in the sermon. Too often we need to take two pictures. They look like this:

Figure 9

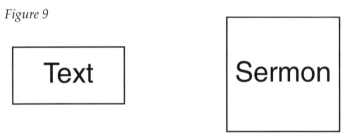

We have a good x ray of the text. We have a good x ray of the sermon—it could be any of the previously mentioned models. But they are on two different pictures. Here's the problem:

The pastors do a good job of studying the text. They may go in great detail to understand the context, the best translations of words and thought. They may have studied hard to gather all of the theological implications of the text. They preach the text that is, from their points of view, a biblical text. But sometimes those who hear the message don't connect it with the text. The pastor has done all of the chewing, and those in pew are expected to do the swallowing.

The good news is the people are getting a biblical message. The bad news is they may think it comes from the pastor or the authority of their own denomination. The message is not transmitted with the text so when they hear the same section of the Scripture again, the sermon is recalled. They have no place to go for further study and no way to transmit it to others by referring to the original source.

The x ray of a better use of the text would show the following:

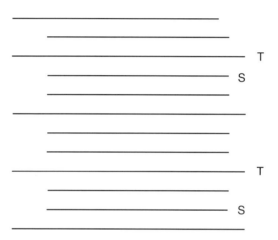

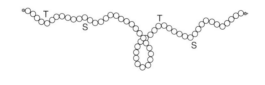

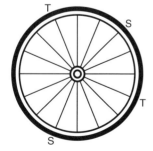

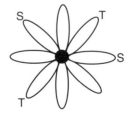

Notice here that the text is used throughout the sermon. The ones in the above x rays are only some of the possibilities. In a theme/parts sermon the text should be used in either the introduction or the theme. Many times each of the parts would include a quote from the text, but that is not always necessary. Each part of the sermon can connect to the text in a different way.

Also notice the *S* on the x rays, which stand for Scripture other than the text. Even though you are preaching a text, other parts of the Bible are often used in a sermon. It is easy to quote words and thoughts from Scripture in a way that the hearers do not know the message comes from the Bible. I think it is a good idea to identify the quote as biblical. You need not give chapter and verse each time, but should be ready to give to those who ask.

In a string of pearls/beads sermon, the use of the text along the way greatly increases the opportunity to find more pearls than beads.

In a bicycle wheel or daisy conceptual sermon the text must be a part of the core. It could be the text is used only in the concept; each idea goes out from the text and back to the core. Or, the idea could go out so the text appears as a part of the loop.

This does not mean the preacher should sprinkle a few Bible verses in the sermon so the message sounds like it comes from God's Word. Bible verses can be misused or can be used in a way that they do not seem to relate to the message the pastor is preaching. The text is God's part of the sermon. We mortals are to get involved, and we need not be afraid to put ourselves into the situations of the text.

Let me illustrate it this way: We do not get top billing on the church sign out front for the sermons we preach. Nor are we co-starring with the Holy Spirit in our sermons. We have a supporting role in the sermon. If we get an Oscar, let's be sure we know whom we should thank.

I also think that a valid purpose of a sermon may be to teach the text so those who hear it will have it as a resource for the tests of their lives. Let me explain this one.

Sometime back I wrote Christian curriculum materials. The format always started with "The purpose of this lesson is. ..." I had to identify why the class should be taught. (By the way, I like that idea and think each sermon should have the same requirement.) My first reason would always be to teach the Bible story or verses that were the basis of the lesson. Editors would always redline this with the explanation that teaching the biblical material was using a resource. The purpose of the class was to teach the message of the biblical section. I learned something as I refined my list of purposes for a lesson.

However, I still beg to differ with those who drew the red lines. For instance: If you give a person a fish, you provide one meal. If you teach that person to fish, you help him provide his own meals for years to come. My application of the old proverb: If I teach people a spiritual lesson, I provide God's Word to their present situation. That's a good for reason to preach a sermon. However, if I teach people to know a section of Scripture so they know where it is and how to use it, I am helping them use the message from God for other situations for the rest of their lives—another good reason to preach a sermon.

One good way to do this is to ask those who hear your sermon to go through the text with you. Point out the verse your are talking about. Having the readings for the day printed in the church bulletin is helpful for this. They can underline sections, make other notes, and take the printed text home to post on the refrigerator door.

Even better, your church can provide Bibles in the pews—or you can really go for it and ask people to bring their Bibles from home. You lose the underline part then (at least for the pew Bibles), but the people gain the experience of opening their Bibles and finding the text. Without making a big deal about it, they will learn if they are looking for Jeremiah but found Ezekiel, they need to back up a bit. Also, with a Bible in hand it is easier to refer to the context of the text. People can easily see what happened before or after the words of the text, especially if they are using an edition that gives headlines to each section.

X Rays of Sermon Illustrations

Again we refocus our sermon x-ray machine to give us a picture of the illustrations in a sermon. The first view shows us a major misuse of illustrations:

Figure 10

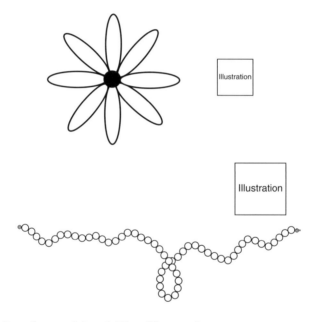

See the problem? The illustrations are not connected to the sermon. You may properly accuse me of being slightly paranoid on this subject, but I'm the one who has written 16 books of children's sermons and am now writing a book about (not of) sermon illustrations. I have the right to be cautious about the misuse of my material.

After I got into writing children's sermons, I discovered that people thought I went around picking up objects and saying, "Aha, there's a message here." Wrong! I spent a lot of time studying Scripture and saying, "Aha, there's a message here." Then I looked for a way to share that message.

Many times we find, or people even give us, good illustrations which are so good they must be used. So we stick them into the next sermon. Listen to other speakers who do it. Use your sermon x-ray machine to catch them. Then learn not to do it.

Let me illustrate:

In a recent editorial William Safire reminded us that in the days of the Wild West the sheep destroyed the range for the cattle because the sheep ate the grass down to the roots. The problem became the plot for many movies. But now a poisonous weed covers much of the not-so-wild West. The weed has ruined the range for cattle. But sheep thrive on the weed. They enjoy it so much they kill it, and the cattle can return to pasture. So the sheep saved the cattle. Safire adds that this true story should be a good illustration for sermons. Thank you, Mr. Safire. But to my readers a caution: The story is an illustration—not a text. Use it when it helps your text.

Another view of misused illustrations in a sermon:

Figure 11

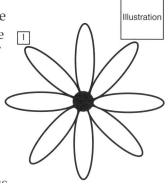

The problem here is the illustration is too large for the point it illustrates. In a theme/part sermon, major illustrations should be for major parts. Each part may have an illustration, but it is not necessary. I heard a theme/four part sermon last week: it was well organized, an excellent illustration was used for one part, no illustrations were used for the others. The effect, which I think the preacher wanted, is that I remember more about the part with the illustration. The illustration was used to give that part of the message priority. Had each part had a similar illustration, the emphasis would have been lost—and the sermon would have been too long.

An oversized illustration is an even bigger problem in a conceptual sermon. The concept itself is the major illustration that can be repeated in each idea. A large but different illustration gives the bicycle wheel two hubs or the daisy two eyes.

In the chapters that follow we will look at a variety of illustrations, some of which will be one word-or-phrase illustrations that can be sprinkled throughout the sermon. The length of the illustration should be in proportion to the importance of the point it illustrates.

X Rays of Motivations in Sermons

Next target of the sermon x-ray machine: the motivation for the hearers in the sermon:

Figure 12

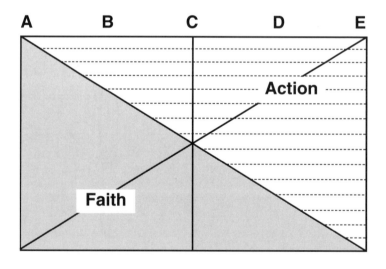

First an explanation of the x ray. I'm going to use two extreme examples with the understanding that few of us will go as far to one side of the figure as I illustrate here.

Some who preach start at point A on the left and preach about faith in Jesus Christ. They tell who Jesus is and what he has done for us. Their goal is to give faith to those who do not believe and to sustain and increase the faith of those who believe. Sometimes they stop at point C or B—or even before and do not talk about the action that comes from faith. The logic, perhaps even theology, is that faith creates action. If people have a strong faith, then they don't need to be told how to use it. Serving Christ comes naturally to those who believe.

This sounds good, but read Scripture. It speaks to believers, yet is filled with directives for action. None of the biblical writers are hesitant to tell us to get to work for our Lord.

Now the other extreme: Some preachers start at point C or D or even further to the right. Their logic, or perhaps even theology, is that people already know who Jesus is and what he has done. They've been taught that—it's in the creeds we use in the service. Therefore the sermon picks up with the believers in the church and heads out the door to the world of Christian action.

This sounds good, but read Scripture. The biblical writers repeat the message of God's promises and the actions of Jesus Christ over and over. These are not just facts that we learn; the Gospel of Christ is the spiritual power to keep us in faith and to get us to work. We need the energy we receive from hearing the faith message in order that we can do the action message.

First, listen to other sermons as you x-ray them on the faith/action scale. Recognize that different texts offer different messages for motivation, and different congregations need different applications. Don't stake out one place on the x ray as the right one for each sermon. Instead look at the x rays of your own sermons. Which extreme are you nearer? Where would your congregation put you on the x ray? Seeing your own sermons from this point of view offers you another opportunity for more variety in your sermons.

BLIPS ON THE SERMON RADAR SCREEN

All art forms have rules, but the rules do not rule the art form. You may break the rules if in so doing you improve the art, but you can't break the rules because you don't know any better. All of this is a defensive action on my part because I'm mixing my metaphor. I'm taking you from an x-ray machine to a radar screen. But I have reasons. See the illustration below:

Figure 13

The radar equipment is located in the pulpit. It sends out beams that continue in space until they hit an object and bounce back to the radar screen as a blip. My point is this:

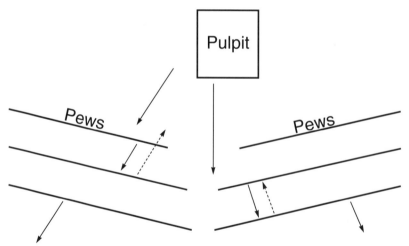

Look at the radar screen of your sermon to see if it is reaching the hearers.

Some sermons seem to stay in the chancel. They have good theology and good structure. They are well spoken. But such sermons can allow the audience to be passive. The only response expected is to agree—which includes the possibility that some might disagree.

A pastor graduated from the seminary and went to an old, rural congregation. Each Sunday he would leave the chancel during the sermon hymn, go to a back room, climb up the stairs, and come out in a pulpit high above the people. He did that every week from August through the Second Sunday of Easter. On that Sunday he read the text from John that tells us Jesus entered a room by going through a wall. The pastor announced, "You have heard about this miracle; now you're going to see one." He picked up his Bible, went out the door, down the steps, back to the chancel, and stood in front of the congregation. I have now walked through a wall," he said. "Now let's share the Gospel of Christ." He preached his sermon.

Had this pastor done the walking through the wall miracle on his first Sunday in the congregation, he probably would have been gone by Easter. First he had gained the trust of his people. They knew he was there because he wanted to share the Gospel of Christ. They appreciated the miracle. There were many blips on the pastor's sermon radar screen.

Your advantage as a pastor is that you preach to people you know and who know you. You can talk to them. They can talk to you. This does not mean every sermon should be a conversation between pastor and people; though that works sometimes in some places. But your contact is not limited to church services. You hear the people throughout the week; they hear you on Sunday. The better you listen during the week; the better they can listen on Sunday.

Dialog sermons were a minor fad 25 years ago. I remember seeing a number of published sermons written by one person but intended to be read (or used) by two: a dialog sermon. I disagreed. One speaker cannot control a dialog. When preaching to a small number, true dialog can occur when people respond to a question or add opinions. Large groups make this more difficult. However, the idea of a dialog can still be used when people are asked to respond in their minds or even to make notes. They become thinking partners in a dialog with the preacher.

As you prepare your sermon, think of ways of sending the beams out of the chancel to the people in the pews. Here are some phrases that I have found myself using in more recent years—and that I have heard others use when I am in the pew.

1. "This is your part of the sermon to work on."
2. "Listen to this list of sins in the text and notice which one causes your blood pressure to go up."
3. "Listen to this list of blessings in the text and pick the ones that make you want to sing the doxology."
4. "How would you answer the question in the text?"
5. "What is your definition of … ?"
6. "How have you included this situation in your prayers?"

Make your own list of ways to let your congregation know you expect them to be listening and their response is a part of the sermon. In some cases you may get a verbal response. Be glad, but make the point that the idea is each person may have a different response. Don't ask questions that expect a yes or no answer.

As you preach the message, remember you are preaching to a congregation. Don't give a message from the pulpit to an individual. Whether the message is encouraging or critical, that should be done privately and is the opposite of the goal I am striving for here. The idea is each listener must hear and apply the message. Don't expect every idea to reach every person, but listen during the week that follows. You will hear blips come up in conversations which are reactions to your sermon. For every one you hear, there are many more you do not hear.

Your Own X Rays

One of the chief goals of conceptual communication is to give an idea and illustrate it, so those who hear can add to it.

If my system works, it is your turn to use the sermon x-ray machine. You will find other ways to x-ray sermons and speeches you hear and hopefully will prepare your sermons with the thought of how they will look on a x-ray screen.

CHAPTER 4

How to Use Conceptual Illustrations

A conceptual sermon (bicycle wheel or daisy models) combines the introduction and an illustration. The concept identifies both the goal of the sermon and gives an illustration to reach that goal. Let me illustrate:

Years ago, a recipe for Starlight Double Delight won the Pillsbury Bake-Off contest. The directions included the following: *Mix the batter in one bowl and a double amount of icing in another. Pour half of the icing into the batter and bake the cake. Use the rest of the icing as on a regular cake. The results are fantastic!* I haven't eaten Starlight Double Delight for about 50 years, but I still remember it. Forget the gooey calorie part—the point is this recipe made a cake that had the best part mixed all the way through it. May it be so for your sermons.

When I was taught the theme/part method of preaching, I was told to prepare the sermon first and then find an introduction. The process is reversed for a conceptual sermon. The first job is to clearly define the concept of the sermon in a way that will use each part of the material. The concept holds the rest of the sermon together. For example:

The concept is a minidevotion complete in itself. In a short time it tells the hearers the basic message. The rest of the sermon applies that idea to specific situations and offers ways to use the message for one's self and to share it with others. The speaker starts with the concept, reaches out to a lesson or application in the lives of the hearers, and brings them back to the concept. Repeat as often as necessary.

The concept is a story or visual that will be the core of the message. Each idea used will start with the idea of the story or visual and will come back to it.

A children's sermon is often a concept which can be developed in the regular sermon. Preachers often discuss how many points a sermon should have. The answer is "At least one." For children's sermons, the answer is "Only one." When the children's sermon is used first, it can give the concept to be developed later—even if the same person does not preach both of the sermons.

Something happened 20 years ago that encouraged me to pursue my efforts at conceptual preaching with visual illustrations. I had accepted a call and the congregation I had served prepared a farewell dinner. One of the speakers for the evening brought in a big box. He pulled a carton of salt out of the box and asked, "What does this remind you of?" The people identified an old sermon. Next he held up a bucket from a fast food chicken restaurant, and again the people identified a sermon. (These two are mentioned because they are used later in this chapter.) After he had shown a number of objects and told a number of stories, others at the party identified other sermons by object and story.

I do not tell this story because I have an exalted view of myself as a preacher. I have many weaknesses—some of which I can admit in print. I talk too fast. My voice doesn't carry well. I have a tendency to get a sentence started and then drop it with the idea that if you are paying attention, you should be able to figure it out. If you're not paying attention, it makes no difference anyway. None of these are good. But I know I have a great message about Jesus Christ. I know I get my message from the best source: the Holy Scripture.

You have the same. I'm sure you also have some limitations as a preacher. We can make that into a blessing. Paul said when he recognized his weaknesses, he became strong. Long ago, I figured out I didn't have a voice that overpowered people. Rather than be jealous of those who have such voices, I decided I'd work on having something worthwhile to say. The emphasis is on the message—not the messenger.

You may think I am pushing conceptual preaching as the highest homiletical method. Think again. I am offering it as one way, and I am encouraging you to find the way that is best for you. The story of my farewell party helped me recognize what works best for me. It is your job, with the help of your congregation, to find what works best for you.

Those who preach to the same congregation week after week (which is the real joy of preaching) need to work on variety. When your organist knows the exact time in your sermon to return to the bench and the ushers know exactly when to look for the offering plates, you have become too predictable. Get a new style next week so you'll be less predictable.

I will give you more examples of conceptual sermons that I have used because I want you to have the illustrations available to you. However, I suggest you use my ideas as a starter set. Use them to get in the conceptual mode. Learn to look for your own concepts in the text and in the lives of the people who hear your sermons.

Often the concepts are given in the text because conceptual thinkers wrote the Bible. The salt shaker sermon below is an illustration of this. Read the text and its context to see what holds the message together. Too often our study of a text leads us to fine details of words or phrases but does not show us the whole picture. Too often we pick up one thought from the text and take it out of context to develop a good sermon, but it does not include the central message of the text. The text is the best authority to help us understand its message. If you buy the idea that a good way to preach a sermon is to introduce your two friends—the text and the congregation—then one way to start is to get to know the text so you can properly introduce it.

The other way is to look for your concept in the lives of the people who will listen to the text. Know them and look for ideas, needs, and events in their lives which will help them understand the message of the text. Many times your concept for a sermon will come from what the people do in their everyday lives. The chicken bucket sermon below is one example.

A sermon that uses the Good Shepherd as a concept starts with the Scripture because people today are not shepherds, and few have ever seen one. The sermon does not teach them about shepherds, but it teaches a concept by showing how a shepherd handled situations.

If you use a concept about a baby-sitter, you are starting in the lives of your people. With the possible exception of Miriam and her little brother Moses, we don't have baby-sitters in the Scripture. Yet there are a number of concepts that could come from the relationship of a baby-sitter with a child and with parents. I'll let you work on that one.

The concept for such a sermon does not always have to include an object or a story. It is what the word concept tells us—an idea. It is a central idea to which all parts of the sermon are attached.

NOW LET ME ILLUSTRATE

The five conceptual sermons listed below are offered as illustrations of the idea. I do not regard them as complete sermons; though each of them could be used as a brief devotion. If you use them for a sermon, it is your job to develop the concept into a sermon for your congregation. You will still need to study the text, apply your gifts as a preacher, and make special applications for your congregation.

From my point of view, the advantage of the conceptual sermon is the concept does not become a canned sermon to be opened and reheated for local consumption. I think you will guess I have used the sermons below many times and in many situations. Each time the delivered sermon was altered because I was preaching to a different group, and because of my own experiences since I had prepared the concept. You will need to do the same.

Let me illustrate: I enjoy potluck dinners. I have noticed that several cooks can use the same recipe, but the finish products are different. (I always like to take a little of each.) If each of the cooks had opened a box of prepared food and heated it, the results would have been the same. But even though they used the same ingredients, they came up with their own version of food that they cooked. Likewise, you can use the resources I am offering you below (and elsewhere in this book) and add your own touch to produce your own sermon.

Concept: Pass the Salt

Text: Matthew 5:13

Jesus tells his disciples, including us, that we are the salt of the earth. Those who believe in Christ are the salt for all people. Something has happened to us because we believe Jesus is our Savior.

Look at this salt. (Use a large container, a very large shaker or, even better, the box of salt from the story.) When Jesus became our Savior, he salted us. He has given us a different flavor. We don't eat salt as a food item. Rather, we add salt to enhance the flavor of food that we eat. The Gospel of Christ is not a separate serving in the banquet of life. Jesus Christ became a part of all human beings; he is a part of all we do. Because of his death and resurrection he has changed us. Since we are changed, we have a different taste in our lives.

Look at this salt container as though it contained the Christian message. Jesus has given this shaker to other people to pass the message of the Gospel to us—to salt us down. (Hold the salt over yourself and others as you give each application.) When you were baptized in the name of Jesus Christ, you were made one with him. Your life was given a new fla-

78

vor. When you read and hear God's message for you in Scripture, you are being salted to taste. Each message adds to your Christian flavor. When you receive the body and blood of Christ in the Lord's Supper, you receive more of the flavor of Christ. When you participate in a Christian community by your worship and your work, you are receiving the salt of Christ from those around you.

Look at being salted in another way. Your life has many different parts. Identify some of them: Your family life. Your job. Your social life. Your financial life. Your sexual life. Your values. Your commitments. Get the picture? Now think of me as standing next to you. I reach out this salt container to salt your life. In what areas of your life do you want me to pour the salt of Christ? Where do you need his love and protection? Where do you need his grace and forgiveness? Where do you need his instruction and guidance? The salt is here. Get plenty of it.

Your presence in church today makes me feel sure you can say no to this question, but I want to ask it. Are you on a salt-free diet? Even in church do you avoid letting the word get to your heart and mind? I ask the question so you will think about it now and not let it happen in the future. I also ask the question so you can understand those who are on a salt-free diet, which brings us to the next issue.

I'm the one holding the salt shaker today, but I'm not the only one around who believes in Jesus and wants to share that faith with you. Think of the people in your daily life. Those who believe in Christ are also the salt of the earth. Can you help them help you? Can you tell them where you need to be salted? Next step. You who are salted become salt. (In some cases you might give each person a small package of salt. If you do, explain it is a symbol. The issue is the salt in the package, not the amount.) People who you associate with every day need this salt. They need to see it in the way you live. They need to hear it in what you say.

Look for ways you can be salt for the people of the world. Start in your family. Recognize the things which cause conflict and arguments. Apply the love of Christ to those issues. Look for opportunities to speak acceptance and forgiveness. Be willing to accept help from others.

Look at your work, school, and other contacts. List your complains and the complaints of others. Then remember the salt in your hand. Do not make the problems worse by adding to the trouble. Let the presence of Christ be there through you.

When you vote, do you consider only your own needs and what will be best for you? Or, can you be salt for other people by considering the needs of those who cannot or will not vote? Can you give salt to others through the workings of our government?

Do you know you can use the staff and programs of our congregation and church body to pass the salt to others?

You may have a container of salt like this in one of the cupboards at home. You have a salt shaker on your table or lunch counter. You see salt on the table when you go to a restaurant. Let each one of these be a reminder that you are the salt of the earth.

It's a Matter of Distribution

Text: 2 Corinthians 5:17–20

The law of supply and demand determines the success or failure of a business. If you have a large supply of an item, let's say hula hoops, but there is no demand for hula hoops, your business will go down the tube. On the other hand, if there is a large demand for an item, let's say fresh strawberries, but a late frost wiped out the strawberry vines, you're out of business.

I'm not here to tell you how to run your business by the law of supply and demand. I want to apply the principle of supply and demand to the business of the church.

First, let's look at the supply. Our text tells us, "All of this is done by God, who through Christ changes us from enemies into his friends" (2 Corinthians 5:18). I am pretending there is a period at that place in the text; there isn't. We'll come back to the rest of the sentence later.

God has provided the supply we need. Think of this bucket (the largest chicken bucket or similar food container available). God fills the bucket. When Paul said all of this, he is referring back to what God has done for us through Jesus Christ. Watch God fill the bucket. He sent his Son to be a human being with us. Jesus lived on earth to be a part of our lives. He was in a family, a community, and a nation. He worked, and he had friends. He was tempted. He cried. He went to parties. He was God living on earth as a human.

Because he was human, he took our problems on him. He was betrayed, beaten, abused, degraded, and killed—all for us. He rose from the dead and claimed victory over sin and death. He sent believers out to tell his message—and they have arrived in our place and our time to give us the message. He has baptized us in the name of the Father, Son, and Holy Spirit. Christ has given us his body and blood in the Lord's Supper. All of this is for all people. The supply is unlimited. Can you see the bucket overflowing with God's grace in Jesus Christ? I put that bucket in front of you. What a supply!

Now let's think about the demand. There are all kinds of religious supplies in the world. There are a number of great religious books that tell us what to do and what not to do. There are beautiful places of worship, great ideas about the brotherhood of mankind, peaceful ways to meditate and reflect on life. But only Jesus Christ has offered to pay for the sins of the world. Only Jesus Christ has died and rose from the dead to give eternal life to all who believe in him. He has a corner on the market.

What he has to offer is needed by all people. All have sinned and fallen short of the glory of God. (See Romans 3:10–12.) It is not true that the only sure things in the world are death and taxes. Some people don't pay taxes. But all people will die because all people sin.

What's wrong with this picture? Look around you. I'm glad you are here. I'm glad that you recognize your need for the grace of God. But if everyone needs what we have to give, and if we have enough to give to everyone who wants it, why is that pew empty?

The answer is in the rest of the sentence—the one where I prematurely put a period. Let me read you the whole thing from the beginning, "All of this was done by God, who through Christ changed us from enemies into his friends [this is the rest] and gave us the task of making others his friends also."

Now do you see the problem? It's not in the supply—plenty of God's grace for everyone. It's not in the demand—everyone needs that grace. The problem is in the distribution. The product we have to offer—you have imagined it in this bucket—is the greatest demand of all people. If you have a warehouse full of hula hoops in Detroit, but the only place where they are still the rage is in Australia, you have to work on distribution. If your customers want strawberries here, but the nearest crop is in Baja, Mexico, you have to work on distribution.

God has taken care of the supply. The world has provided the demand. Now we are given the job of distribution. Because God has changed us from being his enemies to being his friends, he has given us the job of making others be his friends also. The job sounds simple. Just take this bucket and pass it to others. There's way more grace here than you can ever need. God always gives in abundance. Help yourself to all you need—there will still be leftovers. Pass it on.

This is a part of the problem. (Show the smallest chicken box used to serve a single meal.) God serves in the bucket, but sometimes we accept only with a single serving box—just enough for ourselves. Too often we are content to know that we are forgiven, that we will be raised from the dead. That's true. But when you know that truth, you become a part of God's distribution system.

We're in this business together—together in this congregation and together in our church body. First we receive. Then we pass it on. Each of us shares the responsibility of keeping our church in the right business. God has taken care of production—we are operating a distribution center.

You Are an Answer to Prayer

Text: Acts 16:9–10

This story about Paul and the man from Macedonia tells us something important about prayer as a communication system with God. The Macedonian prayed to God. Paul gets the message. At first this seems like a problem. Could the Macedonian pray to Paul? That would never work. Could Paul listen in on God's prayer line? Highly unlikely. Yet the story gives us a picture of a prayer and how it is answered.

Let's imagine God's prayer system from a human point of view. Remember, I don't think this is how prayers are really handled in heaven, but let's use our own communication systems to help understand how God answers our prayers—and just as Paul was, so we also may be an answer to prayer.

First, pretend there is a huge building in heaven called INCOMING PRAYERS. This building is filled with little slots like these. (Have a small section of mail slots like those that were behind the registration desk at a hotel. You can make these with cardboard. Put a sign on the slots: INCOMING PRAYERS.) This is just a small section. Pretend every person on earth has a slot like one of these. This is my slot in the INCOMING PRAYER building. This is yours, and yours.

When we pray, God hears our prayers. Each prayer is put on a little piece of paper like this—remember we are pretending. Then the Incoming Prayer Angels put the prayers in the boxes of those who submitted the prayers. The Macedonian's prayer went into that box. We do a lot of praying in church; so the angels are busy putting the prayers in each of our places. Take a look at your box. Are there any prayers there? Do you have a backlog of unanswered prayers? If I were allowed to take a look at the prayers left in your box, would I know what your priorities are? Would I know what you care about? Would I know who you care about? The prayers in your box would tell a lot about you.

Another thing: We have submitted each of our prayers in Jesus' name. It's marked here on the bottom of each prayer. That means these are not orders sent to God and he has to fill each one of them. When we pray in Jesus' name, we are saying we haven't earned the right to make such requests. We can't tell God we have earned anything in the past, nor can we order something on credit with a promise we'll pay for it later. We pray in Jesus' name because we live by his grace. We who deserve nothing from God are free to ask God for all kinds of things because Jesus lets us use his name. He has paid the rent on our prayer box in heaven.

You can think about the prayers that have been left in your box for a long time. God has many ways to answer a prayer. For most of them he says yes, and we hardly notice. Sometimes he says no, and we remember those. Sometimes he says, "Wait a while." And we get impatient about those. One Christian lady heard that God often answered prayers by saying, "Wait a while." She said, "So I'm 53 years old, and I wake up to find a pony in my backyard."

Let's get back to the text. The Macedonian had a box for incoming prayers. So did Paul. But how did Paul get the Macedonian's message?

Back to pretending again. In another part of heaven— over here—is another big building, the exact size of the first one. This one is called OUTGOING PRAYERS. This building has exactly the same number of boxes as the first one. Again each person on earth has a box in the OUTGOING PRAYERS building. (Show another set of slots exactly like the first but labeled OUTGOING PRAYERS.)

Another unit of angels work in the OUTGOING PRAYER building. Their job is to go over to the INCOMING PRAYERS building, pick up the prayers (go over and do it), and take them back over here. Then they distribute the prayers to all of these boxes.

Here's how it works. Today in the Lord's Prayer we will pray for our daily bread. Our request will be put in our Incoming Prayer slot. The angels from over here will get the prayer and put it in the slots in this section. Think of all the people whom God uses to answer our prayers for food. Start with the farmers, the truckers, the processors, the grocery people, the restaurant people, and others—maybe even some of you here. Or, in our prayers we will ask God to help those who are ill. The angels will take those prayers to someone over here. Just for the record, how many of you work in a way to answer our prayers for medical care?

See how it worked in the text. The Macedonian prayed. The prayer went here. The angels then assigned Paul as the one to answer that prayer for God. We still pray to God. We still get help from God. But God not only hears our prayers; he also lets us be an answer to the prayers of others.

My purpose in showing you these two pretend buildings is to encourage you to check your prayer slots often—both of them. Keep praying to fill this slot over here. Also, keep listening so you know what prayers God has assigned to you over here.

Come to the Grand Opening

Text: Luke 24:1–12

You've seen the signs that say, "COME TO THE GRAND OPENING!" (You might want to have a large banner with that message—better yet, put the message on your bulletin cover or make an insert with the message; so those who worship can take it home.) In the shopping centers you see such signs for weeks, maybe even months, before the grand opening. As the day gets closer, you see the message in the papers or on TV—Come to the grand opening!

Today we are celebrating a grand opening. A long time ago, a blurb about this grand opening appeared in Isaiah 53. After telling his readers the future Messiah would die as a sacrifice to pay for sins and he would be buried in a rich man's grave, Isaiah tells us God said, "After a life of suffering, he will again have joy; he will know that he did not suffer in vain. My devoted servant, with whom I am pleased, will bear the punishment of many and for his sake I will forgive them" (Isaiah 53:11). The Messiah would die—and would have a long life after his death.

Three times Jesus put up the banner "Come to the Grand Opening" for his disciples. (See Matthew 16:21; 17:22, and 20:17–19.) Each time he told them about his coming death, he added that the grave would be opened and he would be alive again.

Apparently his disciples didn't hear the message about his resurrection, because they couldn't believe he would die. But the enemies of Jesus knew he would die, because they helped make it happen. After he was dead, they wanted to make sure he stayed in the grave like a dead person should. They secured the grave with a stone and put a guard on duty nearby. (Show a large, rectangular cardboard box. Display it on its side so the people can see the top—as though it were a crypt. See this as the grave—closed with a stone and sealed tight. (Put a piece of tape across the front end of the box.)

But the grand opening had been advertised. Jesus had made a commitment to die for us—and he had made a commitment to live for us. Our text tells us a group of women who had remained faithful to Jesus even through his death went to the grave that morning. They did not go because they remembered the promise of a grand opening; instead, they carried spices for a dead body. They were concerned how they could move the stone so they could put the spices on his body.

No worries! When they arrived, the grand opening had occurred! (Tear open the front of the box.) The grave was empty. They had worried for nothing. The grave was open. They had wasted their money on the spices.

The story of these women attending the grand opening of Christ's grave is the focus of attention around the world as the sun rises today. Look into the place where they had laid him. (Hold up the box, and let people see that it is empty.) Christ is risen! He is risen indeed!

But that is only part of the story. That was only the beginning of the grand opening. Christ had said before he died, "Because I live, you also will live!" He said that and then died. But he came back to life with the promise that because he lives beyond death, so will we.

Look at the second grand opening of the grave. (Hold the box so people can still see through the open front end. Open the rear of the box and move the box around so all can see through it.) He opened the front of the grave so we could see he had risen. He opened the rear of the grave so we can walk through death to the other side.

To the world, death had always been the end of the story—sin's final victory over us. When we think of our loved ones who have died, we go back physically or in our mind to the grave where they are buried. Each grave is the modern-day version of the gate on the east side of the Garden of Eden; it is the place we have to stop because the angels with long swords stand at the gate and tell us we can't go back to the Garden God had prepared for us.

But today we turn around. We don't look back to the garden of the past, but we look to the place Christ has gone to prepare for us. We do not see angels with swords telling us we can retreat no farther. We look through the grave to the other side. We hear angels tell us, "He is not here; He has been raised" (Luke 24:6).

I want each of you to see the grand opening of this illustration of a grave. The front side is open so we can celebrate today that Christ has risen from the dead. The back of the grave is open; so we know that in the future we can go to a grave in peace because there will be another grand opening when our Lord returns and calls us from our graves.

How Long Are We Going to Keep Doing This Over and Over?

Text: Ephesians 4:30–5:2

Show a dinner plate from an everyday set of dishes. Tell how long you've owned the plate and how many people are in your family. Ask: How many times do you think this plate has been washed? Discuss how often the plate gets dirty, is washed, gets dirty, is washed, and the cycle goes on and on. Why keep on washing the plate? Why not admit that it always gets dirty again anyway, so why bother washing it? Or else, why not quit using it so it never gets dirty again?

The sermon today is not a commercial for some new dishwasher detergent. I'm not interested in dirty and clean plates. I am interested in you; you and I are like this plate. We sin—getting dirty in spiritual language. We repent of our sins, as we have done in this worship service, by admitting our wrong. We are forgiven in the name of Christ, as has happened in this service, and we are clean again. But the story doesn't end here. We will sin again. Repent again. Be forgiven again. The cycle will continue.

How long are we going to keep on doing this? Why not just admit we are sinners and live in our own dirt? Or, why not lower the requirements and decide what we do isn't dirt after all? Today's text says no to both possibilities. Instead, it tells us to continue to fight against our sin. Listen to what Paul tells us to stop. He says, "Get rid of all bitterness, passion, and anger. No more shouting or insults, no more hateful feelings of any sort" (Ephesians 4:31). Notice Paul doesn't give an option here. He does not tell us just to lower our guilt quotient. He doesn't tell us to do the best we can. He says, "Get rid of ..." and I'm sure the list hit each of you. In case it didn't, here are some of the other things on his NO WAY list in the verses before our text starts: No lying. No stealing. No harmful words. If that's not enough, add to the list as it continues after our text: No sexual immorality or indecency. No greed. No use of obscene, profane or vulgar language. Get the message—stop sinning.

But we, like the plate, get dirty. We have to come to be cleaned by Christ again. So do we just keep on sinning because that's the way it is? No. Paul gives us three reasons to fight against our sin. As you listen to these three, I'll also mention some things he does not give us as reasons to stop sinning.

First reason: When we sin, we make the Holy Spirit sad. When we realize how much sin we know about, and that we only know a fraction of the world's sin, we might think the Holy Spirit suffers from severe depression. But the Holy Spirit does not live on a downer; joy is one of the great gifts he gives to us.

We should not fight sin because each sin adds sorrow to the Spirit. We do not teach each sin drives another nail into Jesus' hands. His suffering for sin is done. Do not take the Holy Spirit's sorrow to make you feel guilty. Fire may fight fire, but guilt does not fight guilt. We can't overcome our sin on the strength of our guilt. The Spirit's sorrow shows us the Spirit's love for us. Paul says the Spirit is God's mark of ownership on us to guarantee that we will be free.

We are sorry for our own sins, and we repent. But we cannot repent of our loved one's sins. However, we are sorry. Extreme example: A woman whose 19-year-old son murdered someone told how he came to her to tell her what he had done. She said, "I would rather have been told that my son was murdered than to be told that my son murdered someone else." She loved her son and felt grief for his sin. The Spirit loves us and feels grief.

Many times we have improved our lives because our parents, other family members, teachers, pastors, and others have expected more of us. They loved us and wanted to help us. Put the Holy Spirit on that list of those who love you and feel pain when you sin. You are baptized in the name of the Holy Spirit. He washes the plate that is you and makes you clean.

The next reason you can fight against sin: from the text, "forgive one another, as God has forgiven you through Christ" (Ephesians 4:32). Notice you are already forgiven. That doesn't mean you got away with it. It doesn't mean God didn't know about your sin. It means he did know and he did something to help you: he forgave you. Forgiveness is not permission to sin. Rather, it is giving you a clean plate to start over again.

Notice this text never says, "stop sinning or you will go to hell." That's not Paul's message to the world. He gives a message of forgiveness rather than destruction. The forgiveness comes from Christ; he washes the plate that is you clean. You can start out again.

Next reason, from the text: "Your life must be controlled by love, just as Christ loved us and gave his life for us as a sweet smelling offering and sacrifice that pleases God" (Ephesians 5:2). We have a reason to fight against sin: We are loved by God. Our response to his love is to love him. Just for the record we should admit the desire to be free from sin could be one of the highest expressions of our own self-love. Many times we want to be without sin so we can show we are better than others. We want to look good in the eyes of others. Paul does not give us that as a reason to resist sin. Instead, he tells us to receive the love Christ gave through his death on the cross. Then when we love with his love, we receive the washing he earned when he died to pay for our sins. He put our dirt on his plate and washed it clean for us.

God did not create you as a paper plate—one that gets dirty and is tossed out. God did not create you as an ornamental plate to hang on the wall as a decoration. You are in real life a sinner among sinners. But Christ came to be with all of us in this life. He brings us back again and again so he can clean us. He sends us back to be clean in the world.

Note: When I preached the clean/dirty plate sermon, it was about as you read it above, meaning I adapted it to my verbal rather than written style as I also expect you will do. I want to share three responses to the sermon. These comments from active members of a Christian congregation illustrate how conceptual preaching gives those who hear more than the speaker says:

My problem is that when I recognize my plate is dirty, I put it in the dishwasher, but I don't turn the dishwasher on for several days. The crud on the plate gets dry and moldy. It's more difficult to wash the plate. I've got to learn to operate the dishwasher every day.

Remember that the plate gets dirty only because it's being used as it was intended. If I spend all of my time trying to keep a clean plate, I wouldn't dare be a wife, mother, hold my job, or belong to this church.

Each time I do the dishes I'll think of this sermon and get myself cleaned too.

Concept: God Wears Glasses
Text: Romans 5:6, 11

(In this sermon the concept is explained in the first application rather than an introduction.)

1. God has a problem when he looks at the world. He created beauty, and he sees ugliness. He created peace, and he sees violence. (Develop other contrasts between what God made and what now exists.) We can turn off the TV when we see things we don't like. (Use headlines from a newspaper or pictures from a news magazine to illustrate what God sees as he looks at the world.) We can ignore a few, but not all of the problems around us. But God cannot. God pays the price of knowing all things and seeing all things. God has to see what the people he created are doing. We have turned away from him and from each other. We hurt each other individually and collectively.

2. But our text tells us that God sees us not as enemies, but as friends. This seems impossible. Looking at our record, we realize that if we are his friends, he doesn't need enemies. And that's the idea. God doesn't need enemies because he does not hate. He doesn't need enemies because he doesn't have to prove his power or his authority. God is able to see us as friends instead of ene-

mies because he wears glasses. We use glasses to correct visual problems. God has corrected his problem of looking at a sinful earth by wearing glasses with corrective lenses. Show a pair of glasses. He sent his Son, Jesus Christ, to save us. Use material from verses 6–9 of the text to show what Christ has done. Use a wide marking pen to draw a large cross on each lens of the glasses. These are now Gospel glasses. They are not rose-colored glasses that hide the things we don't want to see. Instead, they are love-colored glasses change what we see because we look through the love that Christ gives to us all. When God looks at us, he sees us through Jesus Christ. Hold the glasses at arm's length and move them around the congregation. God sees you as a friend because in Christ your sin is gone.

3. We also have a visual problem when we look at other people in the world and when we look at ourselves in a mirror. We see the sins of others that hurt us. If we are at all honest with ourselves, we see our sins that hurt others. The Good News is not only that God wears Gospel glasses, but also that he lets us wear his glasses. Put the glasses on. Are you more comfortable if you know I see you through the cross of Jesus Christ? Through these glasses I cannot see any of your faults. They are all forgiven. When I look at you through these glasses, you don't have to explain or defend anything. You are my friend in Jesus Christ. Would you like for everyone in your family and all of your friends and co-workers to wear these glasses? Sounds great. You can do it. Start by putting the glasses on yourself. First look at those people you already love. See them in Christ to make the love secure. Then look at the people who are enemies. God knows what those people have done to hurt you. But he sees them through Jesus Christ and forgives them. He gives the love to you that allows you to see them in Christ also.

Conclusion: We rejoice because of what God has done for us through our Lord Jesus Christ. Because we are now God's friends, we can be friends with one another too.

Note: About a year after I first preached the Gospel-glasses sermon I was part of a building committee meeting as the congregation planned a new worship area. As I discussed an opposing view about the altar with one of the members, I took off my glasses and then laid them on the table. She instantly said, "When you talk to me put those glasses back on." It took me, and the others on the committee a while to connect her comment with the glasses in the sermon.

DEVELOPING YOUR OWN CONCEPTUAL SERMONS.

Most of our sermon preparation is done in private, but the sermon is delivered in public. All things done in private look and sound different when exposed to the light of reality. I have found it helped me to let a group help develop the applications of a conceptual sermon. It works for staff devotions, elders' meetings, or for a special study group. Your job as preacher is to give the concept, then listen to the ways other people apply it to their lives.

CHAPTER 5

How to Use Objects and Visuals

Which works best for you:

1. What is a continuous line on which all points are equal distance from a common point?

2. Or, what is this?

I do not believe a picture is always worth a thousand words, but in this case the picture is worth more than 16 words. We need words to communicate in conversations and in print. Sometimes, we also need pictures. Words often help pictures do their jobs; pictures often help words do their jobs.

Notice how often the printed page uses pictures and charts to help the reader understand the message of the words. Think what happened to communication when the audio of radio was joined by the video of television. In the rush from print to picture, some will always over do it—of course. I once sat in one of those long night discussions in which a young pastor insisted that all words, in print and oral, were of the Law. Words were legalistic. The Gospel could be seen only in action. (His views.) I was getting tired, so I asked the young man—who used a lot of words—to show us the Gospel. He demurred, with the explanation that the objects available limited us. I suggested he use words to describe the objects and show us the Gospel. He finally asked us to see a mother nursing her newborn baby as the Gospel. That ended the discussion. The good news (not capital letters) was we got to go to bed.

After that disclaimer, let's rejoice in the fact that the Gospel is an action. God came in Jesus Christ to die for us, and he rose from the dead. I used words to say it, but you saw the picture and shared the experience. The distinction between print and picture becomes blurred when words are used to help us see, feel, and even smell that which is happening or has happened.

The biblical writers spoke their message long before it was available on the page for readers. Scripture is filled with word pictures, used long before someone thought of illustrating the Bible. I'm going to identify some of the visual aids used by Scripture writers with no thought of giving a full list. These are the ones I have used often—or have seen others use.

1. Jeremiah and his linen shorts—Jeremiah 13:1–11. A friend of mine used this one with visuals on a five-minute TV devotion. I still remember it when I read Jeremiah, 25 years later.

2. Jeremiah and the wine jar—Jeremiah 13:12–14. I used this one and broke a bottle. A member of the congregation scolded me for teaching children to be destructive. I asked her what she thought of Jeremiah. She said he should have known better too.

3. Jeremiah and the pottery—Jeremiah 18

4. Ezekiel and the siege of Jerusalem—Ezekiel 5

5. Amos and the plumb line—Amos 7:7–9

6. Jesus and the seed, the coin, the child, the net, the fish, the bread, the water, etc.

All of the above—and many more pictures—have contributed to the communication of God's word to people. Without the word that gives the meaning to the pictures, the objects listed would just be things. With the word, they are symbols.

Therefore, I believe visual aids *can be* effective aids in sermons to communicate the Gospel of Christ. Not everyone has, or does, agree with this. I asked for permission to write my thesis at the graduate level in the seminary on the use of objects as illustrations in sermons. My request was declined on the basis that object lessons are for children in classrooms, not for adults in church. So 35 years later I'm writing the thesis I wanted to write then. I will admit it may be a good idea I had to wait all those years. This book is far more realistic than my thesis would have been.

However, my first call was not only far from church leaders, but also from members of my denomination. I was desperate to communicate to people who understand my words, but not my accent, and not my faith. I started using visual aids. It helped.

My next call was to a congregation near the Air University at Maxwell Air Force Base. I arrived about two weeks before school started—along with about one-third of the congregation who were students at the Air University. I used visual aids the first Sunday with the idea that new pastors can get away with anything. Then I discovered a good part of the congregation had or were working on master's degrees—often in education, administration, or communication. I worried that I had offended them with my classroom/child methodology.

To my surprise, the Air University students were the ones who started inviting me to lunch to discuss communication, visuals, and conceptual thinking. They encouraged me, taught me, and challenged me. One told me he was so busy he had hoped for a dull church so he could give his brain time off once a week, but it hadn't worked. He said my sermons helped him see things he needed to see far beyond visual aids. Later he died in Vietnam. I treasure my ministry to him, and I appreciate his ministry to me.

Now let me tell you the rest of the story about visual aids. They will not rescue an ineffective sermon. Visual aids are not a substitute for Bible study, hard work, and clear Law/Gospel thinking in sermon preparation. A properly used visual aid will help a well-prepared sermon be understood and remembered, but it will not make the sermon. Visual aids need a purpose. You as the preacher need to know their purposes, and you need to let your hearers know why you are using them.

Let's also recognize that not everyone is able to use visual aids. For some speakers, object lessons get in the way and interfere with rather than help communication. The purpose of this book is to help those who preach find effective ways that work for them. It is not to promote one method. We all have different gifts, and we all lack certain gifts. When you put us all together, we get the job done and the people who listen are glad for the variety among us.

It will be obvious to you that I think visual aids are helpful for me. Some pastors have used my children's sermons by translating my visuals back to words. They found my ideas helpful—but not my methods. That's great. As I recognize my ability to use this method, I also must acknowledge I lack many other gifts. I have no singing ability. During my on-the-job-training year, the pastor I worked for told me I would chant the first line of the *Gloria in Excelsis.* I explained my musical impairment. He told me I'd never learn unless I tried. In desperation I invited him to take a ride out in the country with me far away from people. I told him out there I would be willing to sing the first line of the *Gloria* and he could make the decision. It worked. If someone pushes you to use object lessons and you are not comfortable, don't do it. Tell my music story. It might help.

With those limitations in mind, let's look at the positive uses of visual aids.

VISUAL AIDS AS CONNECTIONS

A sermon needs to connect the hearers to the text and the text to the hearers. A visual aid can help make that connection. The text is an electrical receptacle. The congregation is an unlit light bulb across the room. The illustration is an extension cord to connect the two. Let me illustrate:

1. The text (in my case Psalm 126:1, and 6, but it would work with others) is about weeping and rejoicing. You can connect those thoughts with people today using a happy face and a sad face. Show a large picture of either face when you are reading or speaking about the two emotions. Or, provide a sheet of both happy faces and sad faces to each person who worships and ask them to identify where each face fits in their lives. Tell the story of Good Friday (sad face) and Easter (happy face).

2. Text: Deuteronomy 6:5 or New Testament quotations. God tells us to love him with all of our hearts, souls, and minds. Good idea, but how do we do it. Prior to the sermon, pin a paper heart over your own heart. Also put a small heart in one of your shoes, up a sleeve, in your hair, in your billfold, under your watch, on your car keys, and any other place you can think of. Explain that the hearts represent the love Christ has for us. It comes into our hearts, our minds. His love leads where we talk. His love guides us when we use our time, spend our money, drive our cars, etc. Connect the love of Christ with events in the lives of people.

3. The text of Matthew 13:30 tells us not to divide the wheat from the weeds. Let the expert on judgment, Jesus, do the dividing on Judgment Day. Few of us are into sorting the weeds from the wheat. Connect the text with the people by showing them a bag full of coins—lots of coins. The value of the coins is obvious: a penny is worth one cent, a nickel worth five cents, etc. However, one coin in the sack is a rare coin worth thousands of dollars. But you don't know which one it is. What are you going to do? First, you're not going to spend or give away a single coin because you might lose the valuable one. Next, you're going to ask a coin expert to look through the sack and find the valuable one. The message of the coins and the wheat and the weeds is the same. Our job is not to sort people out. We take them all to Jesus; he's the expert on saving us.

You're welcome to use these illustrations. They could be used as illustrations for one part of a theme/part sermon, or they could be developed into a conceptual sermon. That's your job. My job is not to give you enough illustrations to get your through a church year. Rather, I want to encourage you to look for ways to connect a text with your congregation. As you study the text, ask yourself, "Is there a visual aid which would help people identify with this message?"

VISUALS AS REMINDERS

Remember the suggestion that we preach a text so people can learn that part of Scripture and make their own applications throughout the rest of their lives—instead of giving them a fish, teach them to fish. Visuals are a good way to help people remember a text for future use. To do this, the visual must be from the text itself so the person who sees the visual will recall it when reading the text later on.

The use of salt in the sermon in the previous chapter comes from the text itself. We would not see the salt in the same way as the people who heard Jesus tell the story; we see it in a shaker or box. Jesus was concerned about the salt losing its taste; we are concerned about those who are on a salt-free diet. But the word *salt* makes us see the container and offers it for our use. It is a salty reminder.

If the text you are using gives its own visual, your job is easy, but not automatic. Don't just place the object in front of the congregation for them to see. When you read the text, show the object. When you refer to the subject in the text, point back to the object. Here's a bonus for you: using visuals this way can cut precious minutes off your sermon. Instead of repeating an idea, you can point to the object that carries the message. Let me illustrate:

1. Isaiah 60:2–3 says God will come like a light—many other texts use the same image. Use a light as you read this text. Shine it on people. God's Word shines on us like a light. Sometimes we turn away from the light. We

won't listen to God's Word. Use a mirror to show how the light can be reflected on people who do not see the light. We who have seen the light can reflect it on others who have turned away.

2. The Bible speaks often of gifts. This works with James 1:17 as well as many other texts. The gifts God gives are not wrapped in packages. They're not returnable. To help connect the list of gifts that God gives to people show a gift catalog. Remind people of the childhood game of picking one gift from each page of such a catalog. The Bible is a gift catalog from God. God gives different gifts to different people, but they all come from God. All of us receive the gift of Christ as our Savior. All of us receive his love and grace. Look through the Scriptures to find other gifts. Keep on looking.

3. Look at Matthew 16:19 and context. Jesus gave Peter a key to heaven. The key was not just for his private use. He could open the door of heaven for other people by telling them the Gospel of Christ. Use a key for the building where you are preaching. That key is the only kind of key that will open the door. There may be many copies of the key—but they all have to have the same imprint to open that door. Many people can share the message of Christ. But we all need the key his message made. There is no other key, no other Gospel (Galatians 1:7).

4. In Matthew 13:31–32 Jesus talks about a little seed that produces a big plant. Take note: The rule for the use of visual aids is that they must be large enough to be seen by the crowd that sits in the back row—and the ushers who sit by the wall. However, this case is an exception to the rule. You want the seed to be so little that it is difficult or impossible to be seen. That's the point. Jesus doesn't explain the parable, but we can figure it out. Even a little faith can produce great things in our lives because we believe in a great Savior. The sight of a seed becomes a reminder of our small faith, and of the great results that follow.

VISUALS AS THE TEXT IN ACTION

Visuals may serve as mental strings-around-the-finger to help us remember certain texts, but a visual aid becomes even more effective when it shows the action of the text. The visual as a reminder is a photograph of an idea; a visual in action is a video of an idea. To use a visual this way, you introduce the object or chart and then use the same to show what happens in the text and/or to the people who are listening to it. Let me illustrate:

1. When Jesus used a seed to show how small it was, we just looked at the seed. However, in the story of the farmer planting his crops (Matthew 13), the seed is not a photograph—it's a video. You've got to keep your eyes on the seed because all kinds of things are happening. Birds eat the seeds. Some sprout but don't grow. Some land among the weeds. Some grow and produce a big crop. Here's how it becomes a sermon. Read a simple Gospel text such as John 3:16 or Ephesians 2:8–9. Show that verse as a seed and tell the people you are giving it to each one of them. Perhaps have it written in the bulletin and ask each person to tear it out. All of this should take less than 45 seconds. End the sermon and walk to another place—or better, have the second part done by someone else. Or, you could have someone else do the first part. Now ask the people to evaluate themselves as the soil where the seed landed. Go through Jesus' four-part sermon and let everyone see what happened.

2. In Galatians 3:27 Paul says we put on Christ when we are baptized. Prepare by asking someone to wear a shirt or blouse that can be destroyed or washed. Ask that person to come forward and tear a hole in the garment or mess it up with a marking pen. The damage to the clothing is like our sin. It destroys our usefulness. But look what happens when we are baptized. Put a coat or sweater on the person so it covers the blotch on the shirt

or blouse. Christ has covered our sin. He did not just hide it like done here, he forgave our sins. When we are baptized, we put on Christ. Each day when you get dressed, you can remember you have put on Christ.

3. 2 Corinthians 5:21: Christ is without sin, but he takes our sin away so we can have his righteousness. Give every person an envelope. Ask them to think about their sins and pretend they are putting all of their sins in the envelope. Tell them to seal it. Now, what are you going to do with it? Ask them to pass the envelopes around to each other. This is what we do when we judge one another and blame one another. Notice all of the sins are still there. In fact, we add more when we pass them around. So let's do something else. Ask the usher to collect the envelopes. Put them on the altar. We take our sins to Christ. He doesn't pass them on to others. Instead he pays for them. All the sins we put in those envelopes are forgiven. After church, we'll throw them in the trash. They're gone because Christ took them away. Why keep spreading them around among ourselves when Jesus will get rid of the whole mess for us?

4. In 1 Thessalonians 4:1 Paul tells us to do more and more to please God. It seems he is telling us to do the impossible. Let's check it out. Ask a small child to join you. Ask her if she will do everything you ask. Help her say yes. Then ask her to touch your hand, then touch your belt, then your shoulder, then your nose, then the top of your head. Along the way, the child will not be able to reach the spot. Remind her that she promised to do what you asked. As you discuss why she can't do it, stoop down beside her. Let her touch the top of your head. Point out she can touch your head when you are stooped down but not standing up. As you discuss that, pick her up. See if she can touch the top of your head when you are standing—if you lift her up. God tells us to do things we cannot do by ourselves. But he sent Jesus to live with us and to do these

things for us. Jesus died to pay for our sins and to give us his goodness. He picks us up so we can serve him.

5. 1 Corinthians 15:16–17 and others tell us that because Christ rose from the dead our lives are changed. Want to see how? This is you and I. Show flat paper bag. When God created the prototype of human beings, he breathed in us and gave us life. Blow the bag up. But we messed up his creation. Tear a number of large holes in the bag—not just gashes. Flatten the bag. Now our lives are different. Try to blow up the bag. We have lost the life God gave us. But God sent his Son, Jesus, to live with us. Show a balloon. Blow it up. He also had the life of God in him. But he died on the cross—let the air out of the balloon. Then he rose again. His life with God returned. Blow the balloon up again. That's great—but the important part is that he did it for us. Let the air out of the balloon and put it in the paper bag. Blow the balloon up again, and it will inflate the bag. We again have the life God gave us because Christ is in us.

Not every text offers an opportunity to use a visual involving action. However, it is good to study each text to see what has happened so we can tell the people what is happening. Look for a way to share that message as clearly as you can. You will notice you could use all of the above illustrations without using the visuals and without involving anyone in the action. You could just talk about it. You are the one who has to make that decision for yourself and your congregation. Let me suggest two things for you to consider as you think about using visuals to show action in a sermon.

A. When a commercial comes on TV (use a commercial because they are repeated often), turn your back to the TV and listen to the words. Identify the information you received from the commercial. When the commercial is aired again, watch and listen to it at the same time. What more did you get out of it when you saw it?

B. When I first started writing children's sermons, I was invited to talk about them at a number of pastor's conferences. Many pastors said, "What you said sounds fine to me, but the people in my congregation wouldn't like me to do things like that." Then I started to get invitations to speak to laypeople—Sunday school teachers and church councils. They would tell me, "I wish we could do something like that in our congregation, but our pastor would never allow it." I'm not great on conspiracy theories, but I wonder on this one. Do we use each other as an excuse to dull-down the Gospel? Just asking!

VISUALS FOR ALL THE SENSES

Words work through our sense of hearing, but they can also make us aware of our other senses. Visuals work through our sense of sight, but they can also make us aware of the other senses. Words and visuals together increase the possibility of teaching through all of the senses. Let me illustrate:

1. The Scriptures often tells us about the power of our sinful nature and the power of our new life in Christ— Galatians 5:16–26, for example. Some can lead us to do evil because they know about our sinful nature and appeal to it. Others can lead us to do good because they know we believe in Christ and they help us live our faith. I can control you by what I know about you. For example, right now I am going to make you do something. If you just watch me, you won't even have to listen very much; you will do what I want you to do. Show a lemon and a knife. Slowly cut the lemon in half. Suck on half of the lemon. Because I know that you have salivary glands, I can make your mouth pucker. People who know you are a sinner, can make you sin. People who know your faith, can help you use that faith.

2. James 1:16–18 tells us the way temptation uses our own desires to make us do evil. The danger of temptation is

104

it makes something that is bad seem good. Show a bottle of vanilla. Most of you probably know how good vanilla smells. Take a whiff. Pass it to a few people to verify how good it smells. But have you ever tasted this good smelling stuff? It tastes awful. Like temptation, the smell offers something great. But like temptation, it's not what it seems to be.

3. In Psalm 32:3–5 David tells us the pain he felt when he tried to hide his sin—something like putting a rock in your shoe. Do this as you ask your hearers to remember what having a rock in their shoe feels like. As you walk, remind them of the pain you feel with each step. They cannot see the rock. You can't even see it. But you can feel it. We can hide our sin from others, but it hurts us. When David confessed his sin, God forgave him. Take the rock out of your shoe. It makes living a lot easier when you confess sins and get rid of them.

CHARTS AND GRAPHS

Charts and graphs are good aids for communication. Notice how often advertisements, presidential candidates, and news articles use them. *U.S.A. Today* has made the graph into an art form. When using them in a sermon, you will need a large copy on a stand in the chancel. It also helps to have a copy in the bulletin for people to follow during the sermon— and also to take home. Charts and graphs that have been used in a sermon may be displayed later around the church to keep the image as a reminder to those who heard the sermon.

Let me illustrate the use of some charts and graphs:

1. Text: Mark 9:14–29 with emphasis on the words of a father who wanted Jesus to help his son. The father said, "I do have faith, but not enough. Help me have more!" (Verse 24). By the way, this visual started as a way to teach the relationship of grace and faith in Ephesians 2:8–9; a confirmation student changed the text and

added to the meaning. Figure 1. The assignment is to put them in correct order and show the proper direction on the chart—either God to us, or us to God. One student correctly put grace first and drew an arrow from God to us. Right! Grace is God's gift to us. Then the student put the pencil on "us" and drew this: Figure 2. Faith is our reaction to God's grace. But our faith keeps bumping into all the struggles of life. "I do have faith, but not enough. Help me have more!" When we have faith struggles, we dare not look to ourselves for strength. Instead we follow the struggle of faith back to God's grace to receive Christ's strength.

Figure 1   *Figure 2*

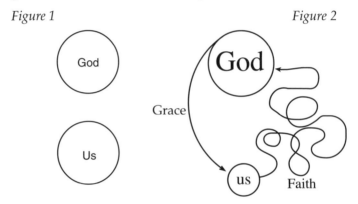

2. In the first part of the Sermon on the Mount, Jesus gives exact details about what we must do to obey God's Law, and "doing" includes what we think. Finally, he sums it up in one sentence: "You must be perfect—just as your Father in heaven is perfect" (Matthew 5:48). Notice Jesus does not define *perfect* by asking us to compare ourselves to one another. Instead, our record must be compared to God's record. Look at this situation on a graph: Figure 3. The top of the graph is perfect—like God is perfect. That's 100 percent holy. At the bottom would be Satan's score. That's 0. Where are you on the graph? We know we cannot be perfect, as God is perfect. Those who claim they are without sin are calling God a liar (see 1 John 1:10). Let's agree the best we can do is 87 percent—

right here on the chart. That's more realistic. Draw a new line across the graph and make that the goal. Do you realize what would happen if we really lower the requirements to our ability to perform? Next year we'd lower it to 83.6. The next year down to 79.1. You see what would happen. In fact, it often does happen. But Jesus still tells us we must be perfect, as God is perfect. So look what Jesus does. He puts his holiness in this area. (Point to the space between our performance and 100%.) Christ not only paid for the sins we have committed; he also gives us credit for the good things we haven't done. He aces the test, and we get the grade. In Christ, remember only in Christ, we are perfect in the sight of God.

Figure 3

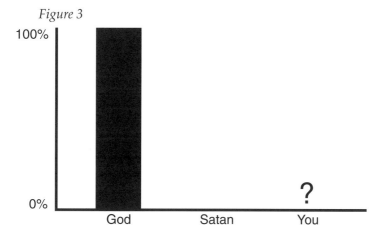

3. Let's stay with the Sermon on the Mount. Beginning in Matthew 6:25, Jesus tells us how to deal with the physical needs of food and clothing—and the abundance of the same. Use a pie graph to help show the problem—and the help. (Draw a large, dark circle on a poster board. Punch a hole in the center and insert five strings—long enough to reach the edge of the graph. Use tape at the end of each string so you can move the strings and change the size of the "piece of pie" that each section makes. Put the following words on thick paper so you can tape each one in a piece of the pie on the

graph: FAMILY, JOB, RECREATION, COMMUNITY, CHURCH.) Use the graph to identify the five major areas named on the cards. Start with family. Talk about the many things that involve your family: homemaking, spouse's needs, children's needs, health, vacation, extended family, etc. How big a slice of the pie does your family need? (Put the word FAMILY on a large slice.) Now your job. Think about all that it requires: going to and from work, things you bring home from work, etc. Put JOB on another slice of the pie. Do the same with each of the other subjects. Put the miscellaneous items under recreation. Define *church* as the institutional church—the time and money you spend that involves the congregation and denomination. Recognize we all have the same amount of time—the pie is the same size for each of us. But each of us has choices about how we divide the pie. We do it every day. A graph like this can make many people feel guilty. Do you think your slice of the pie for your family should be bigger? How about the one for church? The answer Jesus gives us is not a command to give more time and energy to the church. He offers much more. Let Jesus be a part of the whole pie. He is a part of family, job, recreation, and community. Yes, we also need to be sure that he is a part of all we do here at church. When Jesus came to earth, he didn't set up shop in the temple. He included it and the synagogues, but he also lived in a family, had a job, and was a part of a community and nation. When he lived for us, he covered the whole pie. When he died for us, he included every detail of our lives. As we make adjustments on how we use our time, we start with the promise that Christ is with us in all we do.

NOW IT'S YOUR JOB

By putting visual aids into categories, I do not want to limit your use of this method of communication. Don't waste time trying to identify the kinds I have suggested. My goal was to encourage you to see that visual aids have many uses. Sometimes they help and sometimes they hinder the communication. Your job is to deliver the message the best way possible. Because visuals improve communication, they make a good message better, but they also make the wrong message more memorable. Since I am obviously enthused about visuals, I need to show you that they can also fail.

1. The first is an old classic—it may not be true, but it ought to be. A Sunday school teacher wanted to warn her children about the dangers of alcohol. She brought some fishing worms, a glass of water, and a glass of whisky to class. She dropped a worm in the glass of water. It floated around in comfort. She dropped a worm in the bottle of whiskey. It shriveled. "Now what does that teach you?" she asked the class. "If you have worms, drink whiskey," replied one student.

2. The second illustration comes from my family, but enough funerals have occurred to make me free to put it in print. When I was a child in Illinois, illegal slot machines were available in many places, even restaurants and filling stations. One of my notably pious relatives wanted to teach her son never to gamble. She gave him two nickels—remember this was a long time ago. At her urging he used one nickel to buy a delicious candy bar. Didn't it taste good? Then she told him to put the other nickel in the nasty old slot machine to show what a waste it would be. You guessed it! The kid won over 18 bucks.

I have shared the last two examples of visuals to show that even failures have a purpose. We live by the grace of Jesus Christ. When things go wrong, use the mistake as a good/bad example. Remember illustrations do not prove a point; they help us understand something. We must be careful they don't help our hearers understand the wrong things.

CHAPTER 6

How to Use Stories as Illustrations

Sermons and stories belong together. Though both may be written, they are at their best as oral communication. Listen to conversations and see how often we tell stories. At work we tell stories about our family. At home we tell stories about work. We explain ourselves by telling stories from our childhood and from other experiences. We learn about others by listening to their stories.

Recently, I had the opportunity to spend a short week with a couple who were my wife's friends. I thought I knew them slightly, and for three months each winter for five years they had attended the congregation where I served as pastor. I was surprised to find how well they knew me just from the stories they heard in my sermons. These stories, personal or otherwise, showed my faith, my values, my weaknesses, and my joy. Now I've heard their stories too—and we have stories in which all four of us are a part of the plot from the week that we spent together.

Stories told in sermons add another person to the plot—Jesus. Remember the formula for a sermon: introduce your friend the text to your friends the worshipers. Stories help in that introduction, which is why it is very important the stories be both appropriate and be well told. Those of us who preach are to be preachers, not storytellers. Our stories are a means we use to be preachers. Stories used as sermon illustrations are not told for the sake of the story but for the sake of the sermon. A good, well-told story could distract from the sermon if it is more interesting and memorable than the rest of the sermon—and if it has no connection to the text or the intended message for the people.

Let me illustrate: Your text is Matthew 6:24–34. Jesus tells us we cannot serve God and material possessions. Most of the people who hear us preach have a struggle with this problem; it's one of those sins that does qualify for big repentance scenes. We own too much, and sometimes we get distracted in our efforts to earn and keep a balance sheet of assets that we forget our relationship with God. My little sermon to you needs an illustration. A story about King David would help prove the point. As a youth, and when he had to live as an exile, he was faithful to God. He depended on God. When he became wealthy, his life became easy. He didn't go to battle. Instead he stayed home and forgot he needed God. While he was home, he peeked over the wall and saw his neighbor's wife taking a bath. That led David to commit both adultery and murder. The story of David, Bathsheba, and Uriah is a modern soap opera. It makes a great story to tell, but the violence and sex are going to make you and your listeners forget the text about greed as a sin. Either find a different story or leave out the part that would distract from your message.

In this chapter we are going to look at reasons to use stories in sermons, how to use them, give examples of different kinds of stories, and suggest ways for you to find your own stories.

WHY USE STORIES?

In Luke 10:25–37 Jesus has a conversation with a teacher of the Law who asks, "Who is my neighbor?" Jesus answers you are a neighbor to people you help: the message of this section of Luke's Gospel. But Jesus didn't say this in exactly those words. Instead, he used a story to teach the lesson. Then he asked a question. Then the teacher of the Law gave the answer to his own question.

By telling the story, Jesus involved the teacher in the search for an answer to the question. The man had to think about what he had asked, about possible answers, and finally what the answer to his question was. Jesus did not give the man an answer; instead he taught the man to find the answer.

Since that time, the story of the Good Samaritan has been told and retold. Ask yourself how many times you have either taught or been taught that parable. Yet each time you have to deal with the issues again. You have to look at each of the characters in the story and wonder which one is you. Jesus could have given an answer to the teacher of the Law for the man to accept or decline. Instead he gave a story that the man had to live with the rest of his life—and one we still live with today. I'd still like to know if that Samaritan helped everyone in need, or was that just one of his good days. Also—do you think that priest and Levite never helped anyone? Or, was that just a bad day for them? Because Jesus told that story, I still have to think about things like that. Thank you, Jesus.

Stories in the Bible and the stories about those who believe in Christ show our doctrines are not abstract concepts or philosophical opinions to be discussed in ivory towers. When we talk about sin, we are talking about a serious part of the plot in the lives of all people. When we talk about salvation through Jesus Christ, we are saying we have become a part of the story of Jesus, and he has become a part of each of our stories.

Therefore, many stories become a part of the doctrine taught—not only an illustration of it. The story uses words to show the lesson in action. The doctrine is: We are saved by God's grace through faith in the sacrifice of Jesus Christ. The story is: Christ became human to suffer, die on a cross, and rise from the dead to give us eternal life. Through the story we can watch the sorrow he felt in Gethsemane. We can witness the physical and emotional abuse he suffered. We get the picture that sin caused all of this. Then we see the empty tomb, hear angels, and share the experience of being with Christ again. The story and the doctrine are one.

Stories can start from a Bible message and reach out to people of our times. Or, the stories can start with us as we wonder where we are going and build a bridge to the truth of the Scriptures. Either way, the story becomes a method to introduce the text to the people and the people to the text.

Other stories may not carry the doctrine itself. They may be used to introduce the subject, to explain the situation, and to make applications. Follow a thought process here. I have an idea I want those who hear my sermon to understand and remember. I find a story which helps illustrate my idea in the world of the listeners. They hear the story as it is connected with the message. Later they remember the story, and it reconnects their thoughts to the text or the doctrine it illustrated.

Let me illustrate: The story is the envelope first to deliver the message to someone. Then the one who receives the message keeps it in the envelope to pass it on to others.

Notice how Jesus connected his stories to the people who heard them. You know his stories. Check out the questions or situations which caused him to tell those stories. Let me give you just a few:

1. "Who is the greatest?" (Luke 9:46–48)

2. "What must I do to receive eternal life?" (Luke 10:25–27)

3. "Teach us to pray." (Luke 11:1–4)

4. "It is Beelzebub, the chief of the demons, who gives him the power to drive them out." (Luke 11:15)

5. "How happy is the woman who bore you and nursed you!" (Luke 11:27)

6. "They ask for a miracle." (Luke 11:29)

7. "Teacher, tell my brother to divide with me the property our father left us." (Luke 12:13)

8. "Lord, does this parable apply to us, or do you mean it for everyone?" (Luke 12:41)

9. "How happy are those who will sit down at the feast in the Kingdom of God!" (Luke 14:15)

10. "This man welcomes outcasts and even eats with them." (Luke 15:2)

I promised myself I'd stop at 10 examples. You can add to the list. In each case Jesus responds to the situation of people who are listening to him. His stories helped those people, and us, to see how Christ directs our lives.

Notice also how often Jesus starts a story with "the Kingdom of heaven is like …" He is sitting in a most unimpressive kingdom, talking to people who do not look or act like a heavenly choir and he says, "The Kingdom of heaven is like …" Then look at the stories he tells. If we omit the introduction to the story, we can give it a different meaning. Look what Jesus does with his story. He does not describe the kingdom of heaven as John saw it in Revelation. John's vision was for the future. But Jesus was there to help people see the kingdom at that time. The stories show what God does in his kingdom on earth. That's the kingdom where we are citizens for now.

How To Tell Stories as Illustrations

The ability to tell stories is a gift just like musical, artistic, and literary skills. Not everyone can be a great storyteller—and that's not the goal of one using stories as sermon illustrations. However, most people can learn to tell stories effectively. Often it is the effort to become too dramatic or too detailed that ruins a story as an illustration. Some become good storytellers rather than preachers of the Gospel. Some simple guidelines for storytellers:

A story has a beginning, an action, and a conclusion.

I am not treating you like a kindergarten student when I give you such a simple definition. Listen to people who tell stories in everyday conversations. Primarily, stories bomb because the storyteller forgot one or more of the three requirements listed above.

A story needs a beginning. If your story is about a trip from Denver to Atlanta, you start in Denver. You do not tell the interesting details about how you got to the starting place. Nor do you need to tell about all of the problems with luggage at the Denver airport. Save those details for another time. This is why you must know the reason for your story. When Jesus said, "The Kingdom of heaven is like … ," both he and his audience knew what he was going to talk about. We who speak enjoy the details of the story and often make the mistake of including information or "color" that ends up distracting from the lesson of the story.

Speaking and writing are two different disciplines, but they are related. Writing for print has a discipline that speakers need to learn—space limitations. I'm glad you didn't hear the moaning and groaning I have done when some editor has cut paragraphs out of one of my manuscripts. I would point to the red-inked section and explain it was great material. "You're taking something away from the readers," I would say. "Yes," my editor would respond, "and they'll never miss it because they won't know it was there." If the slightest possibility exists that you get carried away in the introduction to your stories, try the discipline of writing the story. Then cut it in half. Then cut it in half again. Cut until you reach the point that every word is necessary.

Just as you can include too much in the introduction to the story, you can fail to include enough. Listen to people who tell stories. Sometimes when they get to the punch line, they realize they forgot to tell you an important detail, so they have to start over. If it is important to know a woman in the story is a widow, then say so. If it is important to know her husband died 20 years ago, then say so. If it is important to know he died in the military, then say so. But don't tell any of those things unless they are a part of the other two elements of the story.

A man took a speed-reading course and was pleased with what he learned. He boasted he was able to read the entire Bible in an hour and 32 minutes. Someone who had seen a Bible but not read it said, "Wow! What's it about?" The speed-reader answered, "God." He had cut out too much.

Years ago my wife and I saw a Dutch version of a folkloric ballet. Each scene started when the curtain rose to show one of Brueghel's paintings. The characters of the painting would come to life as music started. They would dance and interact with one another. When the music stopped, they were all back in place as in the picture, and the curtain dropped.

The introduction to a story is like the lifting of the curtain in the story above. It shows a scene. Then the scene comes to life—that's the action part of a story. Something happens. The action may be a great event such as an earthquake, chase scene, bank robbery, or bankruptcy; such exciting stories get the audience's attention, and remind people of real events. The action also may be a simple thing: a child goes to school; a neighbor drops by for coffee; two men compare golf scores. These kinds of things may not make headlines, but people feel themselves in those situations, or they understand others who have such experiences. We listen to such stories and say, "Been there. Done that." The action in a story need not always include dialog, or even movement. Feelings and senses are actions. The colors of a sunset, the smell of a rose are actions. The storyteller helps those who hear to see and to smell what is going on. Let me illustrate.

1. Walk with me down the Bright Angel trail in the Grand Canyon. We are alone on the trail early in the morning. As we start down the trail, we hear the sounds of wind and traffic echoing in the canyon walls. As we descend deeper, all the sounds from the surface fade away—and there are no sounds from the depths. Yet the silence echoes from the steep walls. It is a silence that makes you stop to listen. You don't want to say a word or to move a rock. The silence is as overwhelming as the best music you've ever heard.

2. In a short story, John Updike starts when the mail was placed in the mailbox at his home. The story follows one piece of mail—a magazine. It goes from the mailbox to the kitchen table, then to the coffee table in the living room. Then the magazine goes into a bucket by the fireplace; then into the garbage can in the alley. I read the story 30 years ago. I know the year because when I remember it, I think it happened in the house where my family was living. There's no excitement in the action of Updike's story; but there are feelings for me, and I wanted to share them with you.

3. A widow went to the temple. That's the scene. She put two cents in the offering plate. That's the action. The story hasn't ended yet so we have to wait to see how it turns out. As long as we listen to and repeat the story, the action phase continues. That lady got a lot of mileage out of her two cents.

Now the final part of a story. The story ends when the action is completed. A story used for a sermon illustration must be limited to the point being made by the speaker. Again, if the story is about a trip from Denver to Atlanta, then the story ends when we arrive at Atlanta. Forget the great shops on Peach Street, and do not take a trip out to Stone Mountain. Those side trips are not a part of this story. If you overshoot the goal of your sermon by adding more, the audience expects another lesson—and the real one is forgotten.

In my story about the Brueghel paintings above, each scene ended exactly as it had started, but something had happened between the beginning and the end. The child leaves for school, the child comes home from school; but a lot has happened in-between. Just ask the teacher.

The conclusion of the story tells the audience why the story was told. The story takes them some place and leaves them there. They need to know where they are at the end of the story. Some people believe there is a special place in hell for those who forget the punch line of a story. Since I believe we are saved by the grace of God through Jesus Christ, I can't accept that judgment. But without that grace, I'd wonder. A bad ending can destroy a good story. That doesn't mean all the details must be wrapped up and explained to conclude the story; often the opposite is true. Read the story of Jonah. From one point of view the story could end with chapter 2. God gave Jonah a job Jonah didn't want. Jonah went the wrong way. God sent a big fish to serve as an underwater limo and delivered Jonah back to where he started. But the story goes on. Jonah does his job and is successful. But God changes his mind about destroying Nineveh when the people repent. Jonah gets mad and pouts. God uses a worm to teach Jonah another lesson. Then what happens? We don't know. Did Jonah finally learn to let God run things? Or, did he still want to serve God as a consultant?

The story ends when it has achieved its purpose. The speaker determines that purpose. That does not mean the speaker controls the outcome. One of the purposes of using stories as sermon illustrations is to involve the hearers in the thought process. Often a question is a good conclusion for a story.

The story needs to be introduced by connecting it with the message of the sermon. At the conclusion, the speaker may briefly mention the point of the illustration again; or may introduce the next issue of the sermon to show the story has now served its purpose.

The length of a story in a sermon must be in proportion to the point it illustrates. In some cases a long story may be used at the beginning of the sermon because it will help understand the entire sermon. If the story is connected only with one part of the sermon, then the story must be shorter. A long story about a minor part of the sermon throws the sermon off balance.

Suppose you have a sermon with three parts. If you think one part is more important than the others, then illustrate that part with a story. The other issues still serve a purpose, but the use of a story helps the hearers remember the more important issue. As I write this, I remember a sermon I heard three months ago. I remember it had four points, but I only remember one of them—the one the pastor illustrated by telling a story about his young daughter. However, that one point helps me remember the sermon, and in a more vague way, the other points of the sermon. Try it when you are listening. Do it when you are speaking.

THE TRUTH IN THE STORY

I have a Bible study I often use called "The Bible as Story." I was surprised one time to find I had offended a woman in a congregation where I was a guest teacher. To her the word *story* meant a lie. Her mother had told her, "Don't tell me any stories." I agree that story can mean a falsehood. I tell you this story (it's true) to share with you the lesson that I have to keep relearning. We need to define our words and thoughts.

Applied to our present subject, it means we need to be aware, and to make our listeners aware, whether our story is told because it is true, because it illustrates the point, or whether it makes no difference. Let me illustrate with two stories:

1. My younger brother died in a boating accident. I was not prepared for the death of a brother—or for those circumstances. It was tough on me. A new member of the congregation came to see me. Though I didn't know her well at that time, I had seen her faith in action. She told me her younger brother had also died a few years ago. She said the experience was very difficult for her family. She gave me no easy answers, but she was there to share with me. I could see that her faith in Christ had helped her through the ordeal. I knew he would also help me.

2. A five-year-old came home from Sunday school and announced that his new teacher was Jesus' grandmother. The boy's mother asked if she had said she was Jesus'

grandmother. The student said no, but he knew she was because all she did was talk about him and show his pictures.

Do you think the second story is true? I doubt it—but it sounds like it could be true. The value of the story is not whether it really happened or not. The value is that the boy teaches us to see Christ as a part of a family. He knows grandmothers. Perhaps he had two. Some kids even have more than that today with all the step-relationships. The story that started as humor also became devotional.

Now look at the first story. It's true as I told it. However, what if the woman who said her brother had died had made up her part of the story? What if she would have said to herself, "That poor pastor is having a rough time. I think I'll tell him that I had a brother die so he won't feel so alone"? The story helped me because it would have been offensive if it were not true. No comfort would be better than false comfort. In that case, the truth of the story is the value of the story.

When we preach, we should never make an issue of the truth of a story we cannot validate. Jerry Falwell once told a story he claimed was true on a national TV program. When someone showed him the story was false, he responded, "We preachers have a right to fib a little to prove a point." No, we do not!

This does not mean that the true vs. false issue is a part of every story used in a sermon. You need not make an issue of it unless you want your audience to know it is true, or if it is a parable or other made-up story. In most cases, the difference is obvious.

Even true stories evolve as they are passed from sermon to sermon. For example, the story I told above about Jerry Falwell. It is true in the sense that I heard it. However, I put words in quotes and attributed them to the televangelist. I realize those may not be the exact words that he spoke. In fact, I deliberately left out the fact that he identified himself by his denomination. I do not think he was fair to other pastors in his church body. When I tell the story, I tell it as something I remember hearing. Putting it in print now made me more aware I need to be careful about not misquoting someone.

Let's see how Jesus used stories to illustrate his message.

1. Sometimes he appealed to common sense. A good tree bears good fruit; a bad tree bears bad fruit. That's true by definition. Someone might want to argue the point. There was this rotten, old, apple tree that gave me the best apples I've ever eaten. I think Jesus would have responded, "Get with the program." He is not teaching a lesson in horticulture. Be aware that some people listen to each detail of a story as though the story were the lesson, not an illustration of a lesson. You need not defend your story on each point. Let common sense prevail—at least on your side of the discussion.

2. Jesus taught lessons based on true events. Check Luke 13:1–5. He uses a current event—the death of 18 people killed in Siloam when a tower fell on them—to prove a point. Those who heard his story knew about the tragedy. It helped them understand his message. The truth about something that happened in Siloam helped his disciples learn a truth about something in themselves.

3. Another story that must be based on a true event from Luke 5:17–26. Some men bring a paralyzed man to Jesus to be healed. Jesus forgives the man's sins. How's that for a change in treatment plans? The people say Jesus does not have the authority to forgive sins. So Jesus heals the man. Go figure. If he has the power to heal—and they knew that was true because they had seen it, does he not also have the power to forgive sins? If the healing is a symbolic message, so is the forgiveness. If a paralyzed man could walk again, a sinner was forgiven.

4. Jesus tells some stories that are deliberately not true. Look at Matthew 20:1–16. Those who worked one hour got the same wages as those who worked all day; the

point being this is not the way human employers work. This is a "The Kingdom of heaven is like …" story. It is true in our relationship with God because we live by grace; but it is not true in the kingdom of the AFL-CIO. I have heard people use this story to argue union/management issues. Time out! This is not about negotiations. It is about one who wants to give what he has—and claims a right to give to everyone without regard for merit. Sounds like heaven to me.

5. Jesus' two most famous stories, the Prodigal Son and the Good Samaritan, may or may not be based on actual events. Both are true in the hearts of people who had a child run away from home, and of those who are faced with the issues of helping others in need. To argue for or against the truth of the stories would be one way to avoid the confrontation with reality that both demand.

6. Just for your enlightenment, read the story of the rich man and Lazarus again in Luke 16:19–31. It is a true story or a parable? The text doesn't tell you. It makes no difference. It could be a true story Jesus tells us to illustrate a point. Or, it could be a parable Jesus tells us to illustrate a point. Either way we learn the same lesson. To spend time in a sermon trying to prove that it is either a parable or an event in history distracts from the meaning of the story.

USING BIBLE STORIES AS ILLUSTRATIONS

A Bible story as an illustration is different than a Bible story as a text. As an illustration, the story helps the audience understand the message of the text. A number of good reasons for using Bible stories as illustrations in sermons follows:
1. Sadly, many people do not know many Bible stories. The only time they hear those stories is in a worship service. One of the reasons for using assigned readings for each Sunday of the year is that the system repeats selected

and important stories. Those who go to church hear them, even if they are not used as the text for a sermon.

2. Bible stories are already part of the plot of your sermon. The Bible is not a collection of unrelated stories. All of the stories relate to the plot: God created us as his perfect people, but we sinned and destroyed the relationship. God promised to renew the relationship and worked through the lives of many people to show his love for us. He sent his Son to become human so he could remove our sins and restore our relationship with God. There are numerous subplots and individual applications, but it all fits together as one story. Read *The Book of God* by Walter Wangerin, Jr. (Zondervan, 1996) for help in telling all of the individual stories as a part of the one story.

3. Stories about biblical characters make good illustrations because they are not divided into those who wear white hats and those who wear black hats. They are all people—they have faults and they have virtues; therefore they have struggles. That sounds like you and me. Those who hear the sermons will have the same reactions.

4. I'll concede this is a minor point, but even a minor point can have value. People who spend any time in art museums need to know Bible stories. I am amazed at how much art is related to biblical characters and issues. If you use Bible stories to illustrate a point, the museums will keep the idea going.

5. If you accepted that minor point, I'll add one more question, "How can people who don't know the Bible work crossword puzzles?"

Now that I've presented my opinions that Bible stories make the best sermon illustrations, let me give a word of caution. The same rules about using other stories as illustrations must apply to those from the Scriptures as well. Just because the story is from the Bible does not make it a part of your sermon. You use the stories, as you use scriptural texts, to help the audience understand and use the message of the sermon. Many Bible stories are so interwoven with other stories (because they are all a part of the same plot) you may be tempted to tell too much of the story.

The other big problem with using Bible stories is you may assume people know the background when they don't— or you may assume they don't when they do. This is one of the dilemmas that we face each week as we prepare sermons for those who have attended church every Sunday for longer than we have lived, and for others who come for the first time and think Jesus is a taxi driver from Mexico City. I have found this a good tension in my sermon preparation, and I trust you to struggle with it also. I have three guidelines—you may have others.

1. People who already know the stories are my partners in ministry. I trust them to appreciate the fact that together we want to teach them to others.

2. We may learn a new lesson each time we hear a story from the Bible because we live in a new situation and know others whom we did not know before.

3. We sing the same songs over and over, and no one complains—at least not many. Why can't we also tell the same stories over and over?

Finally, when you decide to use a Bible story as an illustration in a sermon, it is a good idea to read it again before you tell it. Then tell the story in the language and style of those who will hear it.

HUMOR IN SERMON ILLUSTRATIONS

As one who spent a good part of my ministry preaching and writing children's sermons, I am now going to find some fault with the misuse of them. I'll admit I may be too sensitive on the subject, but it bothers me when I hear pastors and/or congregations reporting that the children's sermon was successful because everyone laughed. The good side is it showed the people were listening, and that is a plus for children's sermons. The bad part is the purpose of a sermon, even humor in a sermon, is not the laughter.

I start this section with a word of caution so that we recognize the problems of misused humor, then clean up our act and use humor in a positive way. All of us are probably closet stand-up comedians and poets. The sound of laughter as a response to something we have said appeals to our egos. I once heard someone speak from the pulpit and tell the people it was okay to laugh. If we need to laugh by permission, we might as well hold up applause signs as they do in the warm-ups for TV sitcoms. Laughter must be a free expression of humor and joy.

Nowhere in your sermon manuscript should there be a note, on paper or mental, that says, "Pause for laughter." If the speaker expects laughter and doesn't get it, the illustration bombs. For the want of a laugh, the illustration is lost. For the want of an illustration, the sermon is lost.

Another concern about the misuse of humor in sermons: A sense of humor does not mean the ability to tell jokes. I have read that many comedians do not have a sense of humor in everyday life. They are professional joke tellers. In my opinion (which means I wouldn't argue the point), stories about the pastor, rabbi, and priest playing golf or fishing do not belong in a sermon. Jokes told as jokes belong in places or situations of entertainment. Illustrations that may be funny are used in sermons.

My last be-careful-about-using-humor warning. Humor can be mean-spirited. Many times we use humor to degrade other people. Because humor is effective, mean humor is a sharp sword. It is the art form of the editorial cartoon. Be careful about humor that may be racist, sexist, a put-down on the handicapped, politically prejudiced, and degrading to other Christians or religions. The story may have a good point, but the negative impact could destroy the purpose.

If the story is the best way you know to illustrate a point, consider acknowledging the possible misuse and turn the negative into a positive. I'm going to try to illustrate this now—even though I am aware I will deal with sensitive subjects. If I fail, I trust you to learn from my mistake. If I get my point across, see if you can do even better. As you read these stories, you will know some of the language has been changed from the way I first heard it. This change was not forced on me by an editor; I have no big desire to be politically correct. But I do want to be sensitive.

1. In the early 1960s, a black man worked on a white man's farm. As they worked together one day, the white boss said, "I had an awful nightmare last night. I dreamed I died and went to the black people's heaven. It was terrible! You should have seen it. The streets—they weren't even streets—just dirt lanes with mud holes and kids everywhere stomping through them and getting everyone dirty. The houses, if you could call them that, were up on stilts with people sleeping under them. People sat on the rickety porches and hung out the windows." The white boss continued to describe his view of heavenly poverty. Finally, the black man said, "You know, boss, it must have been something we ate because I dreamed that I died and went to white man's heaven. It is wonderful! The streets are as wide as from here to that barn over there. They're covered with gold—I mean the real stuff. That gold must have been three inches thick. The houses were big white mansions. The numbers on the house were made out of diamonds. Well, some were only rubies and things like that, but they all looked good. The grass is all mowed and flowers were everywhere. But, you know boss, there ain't a soul there."

2. A pastor who fought in the Revolutionary War and who lost a son in the War of 1812 was angry with the British. In every sermon he found a way to degrade all English people. His elders told him that was all in the past and

he had to forgive. They made him promise he wouldn't say anything against the British in his next sermon. He agreed. His next sermon was on the story from Maundy Thursday night when Jesus told the disciples one of them would betray him. One by one the disciples asked, "Lord, is it I?" Finally Judas said, "I say, old chap, is it I?"

3. A man who became a well-known Christian writer and radio personality told a story about his time as a parish pastor. His congregation grew, and he was highly regarded in his community. A man whom he did not know well, but who came to church regularly, dropped by his office without an appointment. After a little chitchat the man asked, "Pastor, is there anyone in this church who can tell you when you're full of it?" The pastor thought a while and said, "I don't think so." "Then you're in trouble," the visitor said and left. Then the pastor realized he had been wrong. There was one who could tell him.

4. We pastors do not have to get angry and use bad language when someone cheats us or lies to us. We have other ways. For example, when a mechanic accidentally gets grease all over the seats of your new car, you can just say, "I'd like to do you a favor sometime. If your parents want to drop by my office, I'd be glad to marry them for free."

5. The text is James 1:13–15. It tells us temptation grows in us so the thoughts lead to action. The problem is thoughts often seem innocent, but the actions are disastrous. The story: A man was talking to his pastor about his temptations. The pastor asked, "Do you have trouble with sexual fantasies?" The man answered, "No, I rather enjoy them."

Each of the above stories could offend some people, but they could also be used in a way to help many people face reality. Humor has a better chance of getting through our armor of denial than a head-on attack. I have made a drastic change in my final story for this section. I'm embarrassed about the change because it proves I am one of the targets of its humor. But I want to tell it because it does hit me as well as most people *while* they are in church; though at other times it wouldn't raise an eyebrow.

A speaker to a group of Christians reported that half of the world's population suffers from malnutrition. "That's a problem," he said. "But the bigger problem is you don't give a crap that they are suffering. And the biggest problem is you are more upset that I used the word *crap*, than you are that one out of two people in the world does not have enough food to eat." Ouch!

Now let's look at some good reasons to use humor.

1. Humor is a humanizing experience. If someone tells you that you have a good sense of humor, it is a compliment. Politicians use self-effacing humor to react to criticisms. Humor defuses an issue and prevents explosions. We are more relaxed around people who smile and who make us smile. Humor from the pulpit helps break down the wall clergy and church members sometimes build to protect themselves from one another.

2. Humor helps us deal with serious emotional issues without becoming depressed. To help people, we have to deal with a world full of sorrow. We need to walk with people through the valley of the shadow of death. We need to cry with people. We can do that because we can see beyond the shadow of death. We know God has promised to wipe away all of our tears. There is a time for sorrow and a time for joy. (See Ecclesiastes 3:4.) We can help people through the sorrow if we help them laugh. If they learn to share the joy of life with others, they can also share the sorrow of life with others.

3. Humor helps us remember a story or event. Years ago I was teaching Sunday school teachers the story of Gideon, a classic wimp. As I started to tell the story, I

asked them to imagine Don Knotts (I told you this was a long time ago) as Gideon. All I did was read the story, and the teachers laughed all the way through.

4. Humor can be subtle and make people think. Over 35 years ago I preached at a youth rally. I told the story of Nathan Hale's brother Notso. Nathan Hale said, "I am sorry that I have only one life to give for my country." Notso said, "I'm sorry I'm busy now. Catch me later." I used other contrasts between the commitment of Nathan and the selfishness of Notso. The application was that Christ was one who gave his life for the world. He calls those who believe in him to a life of commitment. Never once did I refer to the brother as Notso Hale, but some of the kids got it. I'll admit that it may have gone over the heads of many. But those who got it had something to chew on—and the rest may still have learned something from the story.

5. Humor can make a story or an idea come alive. I was preaching on a text from John's gospel that included a "Verily, verily." President Nixon at that time was famous for his outstretched arms with two extended fingers on each hand. I used his pose and read the "Verily, verily" as, "Let me make this perfectly clear." I would not remember my attempt at humor but for the reaction of a teenager in the third pew. He always had that classic adolescent expression that said, "I'm here but I'm not listening." He broke into a huge grin, then saw me catch his eye. He went back to the blank look, but I knew he was listening.

Humor is an attitude woven through a sermon. That attitude allows an illustration that has a funny punch line because it fits the emotional atmosphere of the sermon. The best humor comes from the situation established for the sermon.

I had always been troubled by Psalm 2:4, "From his throne in heaven the Lord laughs and mocks their [those who are planning a revolt against him] feeble plans." I didn't like the idea of God laughing at me or anyone else even when we are wrong. A three-year-old girl taught me to understand God's humor. Her parents are personal friends; so she knew me by my first name. She was not a morning person, and her parents made the mistake of bringing her to the 8 A.M. service. I had the children's sermon and invited them up. She stalked to the front of the church and announced in a loud voice that I envy, "Eldon, I'm mad at you."

Had any adult said that to me in front of the congregation, I would have been deeply hurt. But, with the congregation, I laughed. I laughed because she didn't intimidate me. I didn't laugh at her, but because I understood her. I had no fear of her anger. I wanted to pick her up and hug her—even though she would have joined a revolution against me. Later I checked Psalm 2. God can laugh at us because we don't scare him. Despite all the stupid things we say and do, he wants to pick us up and hug us. Then, by the way, he straightens out our act, just like my young friend's parents did when she got back from the children's sermon—and just like God did in Psalm 2.

Humor helps us see ourselves. People often laugh when they are reminded of their failures—we call that sin. They are not making light of the sin. Rather, they are saying, "You got me." True story: A couple who had been married 75 years were interviewed on TV. The emcee asked them if they had ever thought about getting divorced. The woman answered, "No, never. But I did think about shooting him twice." The denial of ever thinking about a divorce seemed a little pious—but in their generation it was probably true. However, when the wife admitted her murderous thoughts, she suddenly became real. To admit I understand that says something about me. I used the story in the sermon. The congregation responded with laughter. I told them I accepted their laughter as a confession of sins, and I announced the absolution through Jesus Christ. This story continues the lesson from my little friend who was mad at me. Because Jesus Christ has died for us, we can afford to laugh at sin. That does not mean the sin is not serious—it is damned serious. But we have a Savior; sin does not intimidate us.

Grace invites humor. The funniest stories are those that have a surprise ending. When it didn't happen the way we thought it would, we laugh. Sinners like us are going to heaven. Dead people will rise from the grave. The message brings tears of joy—and sounds of joy.

In the Dark Ages a group of monks were traveling by foot through the Alps. A bad snowstorm came up and they were lost. They were sure that they would die when they happened upon a monastery. They went in and recognized the monks as an order who had taken a vow of silence. Without explaining their situation, they joined the monks in Compline. When the hosts sang the *Te Deum*, the travelers broke into laughter. The message of the psalm and the reality of their deliverance overwhelmed them. They had to laugh.

Some time ago, I read a book review (not the book) that was a dissertation for a Ph.D. on the subject of dirty (as in sexy) stories. The author listened to all the dirty stories available and divided them into categories. He came up with several conclusions about why people tell and listen to such stories. The main reason (or perhaps the one I remember) is people have to talk about sex, but there are very few places people can have an honest conversation about the subject. It is too personal, and there's a fear that others will think you are hitting on them—or you think others are hitting on you. Therefore, we use jokes to talk about the subject. The unfortunate result is that many people believe the misinformation from the stories.

Mary McCarthy wrote a book called *The Group* years ago. During an interview on TV, she was asked why she treated sex as she did in the book. Her response: True sex is a personal, private act between one man and one woman with no camera or reporter present. Therefore, no art or literature has ever portrayed sex accurately. She said the only option available was to present sex as dirty, which it is not, or funny, which it is not. Since then I have read some sex education books and found a third option: dull, which it is not.

The point for us is that humor helps us introduce subjects that are otherwise difficult. What is true about sex is also true about death. Think of how many funny stories you know about death and funerals—and most of them are true. We can often use them to educate, to comfort, to release emotions, and most of all, give a way to talk about death. Let's look at one such story. It comes from one of my seminary classmates.

After the funeral for an elderly man, family and friends gathered at the home where he and his wife had lived for over 50 years. She was in poor health, so visiting nieces searched through the strange kitchen to find dishes to serve snacks on the front porch. In the best of tradition the group sat eating, drinking, and talking. Someone asked the widow if she planned to stay in the house. She answered, "I don't know. Everything I look at reminds me of Henry. Take that glass there. (She pointed to her out-of-town sister-in-law who had just sipped her lemonade.) Henry put his teeth in that glass every night for 30 years." Humor is a part of life. Sermons need to deal with real life.

WHERE TO FIND STORIES FOR SERMON ILLUSTRATIONS

There is no shortcut to find appropriate stories for sermons. Check any book of sermon illustrations and you will find most of the items are stories. However, a good story is not appropriate unless it helps understand the sermon. The search for all illustrations comes at the end, not the beginning, of sermon preparation.

I have used many stories in this book. Each of them is from me to you—not from me to those who hear your sermons. I have told you these stories to help you see my message about the message. If my illustrations help you as you are working on sermons, my job is done. If you can use any of my stories in your sermons, that is part of your job. I have changed many of these stories from how I heard them or how I used them previously. They were changed to fit the needs I have to communicate to you. You must make your changes.

I hope my stories and illustrations serve as a starter set for you as you look for your own illustrations. I'm going to suggest some places for you to look to find stories to use in your sermons.

STORIES FROM YOUR OWN LIFE

I was taught I should never talk about myself in a sermon. We are there to talk about Jesus, not ourselves. I have a different reading on that now. When I got into using object lessons, I discovered that I was an object lesson. I am a sinner—and I know it. Christ died for me—and I believe it. Many times my greatest witness has been my own repentance and faith. The same is true of you.

This does not mean that we use the pulpit for group therapy as we purge ourselves in public. Nor does it mean we use the pulpit to promote our own social, political, or cultural agendas. Instead:

1. Tell your own story as a way to help the listeners to remember and apply a story in their lives. Think of the stories that I have told you about my preaching experiences. They come from the things that have happened to me. In some cases you have had the same experiences. If so, you can react, "Hey, I understand that!" In other cases, you have not had the experience but you can learn from mine. Experience may be the best teacher, but it is also the most expensive. Better that you should learn from someone else's. In other cases, you will remember a different experience by which you have learned something I don't know. My idea helped you only in that it made you go beyond me. All education is aimed at helping the student outlearn the teacher. All of the above can be true as you tell your stories to your congregation. Use the stories to invite people to find and tell their own. Bonus point: They'll often tell you their stories and your supply increases.

2. Your stories will help show both you and your congregation why you view things as you do. Your personal perspective is valuable—it helps you understand a text in real life. However, you need to understand, and you need to tell the hearers, that you may have a different perspective because of your own experiences. This week I heard a man whom I didn't know give a report about a large church gathering. He started by saying, "Maybe you need to know a little about my background to understand why I saw things as I did." He then briefly told about his experiences in the church. Later, as he spoke about some difficult subjects, I could see why he felt the way he did. But he had also helped me understand other people would have reported the same events in a different way. He did not argue to prove he was right, but he told us why he thought as he did. My wife and I have three sons and tried to adopt a daughter. We found ourselves in a catch-22 because every list included someone who was childless. During that time, and perhaps today, my views on abortion were influenced by our inability to adopt a child. That may be good—but I need to explain my attitude and listen to others as they tell their stories. Bonus point: Think about the stories about yourself that you often tell in sermons and Bible classes. You'll learn a lot about yourself—just as those who have heard the stories learned about you.

3. Stories about yourself give a chance to use an I-for-an-eye attitude with people. Trade in the I that is based on ego for the eye that tells how you see things. I visited a Bible class taught by a pastor who was new in that congregation. Several members of the class had different views about a passage from Scripture. I thought they presented their views in a good way and they helped me understand the lesson. However, the pastor insisted that his view (I message) was the correct one. When one person persisted, the pastor explained, "I have been to the seminary so I think

you should accept my answer." I think he could have explained why he saw (the eye message) the text as he did, including what he learned in the seminary.

4. Properly used, stories about yourself help you think of others as they apply the story to themselves. Personal story: I have always been bivocational. For most of my ministry, I was a pastor who wrote on my days off. For over four years, I was a writer who preached and taught Bible classes most weekends. I retired a year early to go back to full-time writing—and there I sat at a computer. I miss the instant feed-back of preaching. As a pastor I was free to tell my stories on Sunday morning because I listened to their stories all week. As I write my stories, I think about you and your congregation. I want my efforts to help you keep focused with eyes and ears on your people.

Examples of my personal stories are throughout this book. If they have made you think of your own stories, they worked. If I have overdone it, you've learned not to make the same mistake. I want to share one more way to use a personal story to help others tell their own. The following was a part of a sermon and was printed in the order of worship.

THE SECOND SECOND ARTICLE

I believe that Eldon Weisheit
    was born of Harry and Edna,
was reborn by the washing of Holy Baptism
in the name of the Triune God,
was married to Carolyn
    and became the father of Dirk, Tim, and Wes.
He is a member of Christ's church,
    a citizen of the United States of America,
    a pastor, and a writer.
He lives as a sinner saved by grace—
    and he will die.
He will be raised again to life by the
    power and promise of Jesus Christ
    with whom he will live for all eternity.

What does this mean?

I believe that my life was created by God and has been redeemed by Jesus Christ so that I might share in the lives of others. I have been blessed by my relationship with God, family, church, and nation—so that I am able to be a blessing to them and others.

Though my sin disrupts each relationship, Jesus Christ has removed all guilt and every excuse for division between me and others. The Holy Spirit has given me faith to receive Christ's gift so I may use the abilities and opportunities given me by my Creator.

Therefore, I live my life, knowing that my failures and inadequacies help me understand the needs of others, so that I may also share the grace of Christ with them.

And I look forward to a Christian death that will remove the barriers of this life, so that I may live forever with Christ and all who believe in him.

This is most certainly true.

The bulletin also included a blank outline for each person to write his or her own Second Second Article. About a year later, a man in the congregation died. As a part of his funeral arrangements he had left his Second Second Article.

STORIES FROM BOOKS OF SERMON ILLUSTRATIONS

You may think that I have bad-mouthed books of sermon illustrations. My problem is not with the books, but with the misuse of them. From my experience, too many of the stories are about holy men taking long walks, or about kings and generals doing the things that kings and generals do; none of which is a part of our lives. These stories do not come from the text, from your life, or from the lives of the people in the pews. I am glad when someone makes good use of such stories—and it can be done. The stories must seem creditable to make their lesson creditable.

Let me illustrate. In chapter 2 I repeated a story that I remember hearing in a sermon years ago—the one about a cheap gift from royalty. When I reread that chapter, I realized I had changed the story—because I had learned something about stories as illustrations. In the original story the man had received the ring as a gift from a king. That doesn't work for me. Notice I changed it to a man's mother who had worked for royalty a long time ago. That could have happened. I can relate to an ancestor who washed dishes for royalty better than to a man who got a ring from a king.

Next, in the story about the man who was prejudiced against the British, I heard it as a case of out-and-out prejudice. The man was too bad to be helpful to me. So I changed the story to include two wars with the British. Even though the man's continued prejudice was wrong, I could have empathy with him—and learn from him.

The best test for a story is to ask, "How would I tell the story to someone while I was waiting for a meeting to start?" Would it fit in a conversation? Would it sound as though I had drifted out of reality? The answers are not in the story from that book of illustrations. It is your job to connect the story with the text and the people.

Let me make something good (in my opinion) out of a holy man taking a long walk. This man was tired of the town where he had lived all of his life. It was Dullsville. So he set out on a trip to find a better place to live. He walked for days. Each night he would sleep along the road. When he took off his shoes, he would point them in the direction he was going. One night a prankster (not an evil spirit) turned the shoes around. That day and the following days the man continued to walk. He came to a place that was familiar. People called him by name. He didn't have to ask for directions. Home was a wonderful place after all.

Remember the game "gossip" that we played as teenagers? I think some groups called it telephone. One person would whisper a message to another who would pass it on to the next. The message was passed around a circle—and always came out much different than it started. If we traced down all of the stories in sermon illustration books (included those in this book), the stories you have heard in sermons and the stories you have told in sermons, it might all be one big game of gossip. Each of us has changed the story. That is good if we made the change to help make the story understandable and helpful to those who hear us tell it in a sermon. Reminder of a caution made earlier in this chapter: Don't mess around with a story that you tell to be factual.

STORIES FROM YOUR CONGREGATION

Stories from your own congregation can be the best, or the worst, illustrations in your sermons because the people understand the situation and are often a part of it.

However, no story from the pulpit should be embarrassing to a member of the church and should not even hint at revealing something confidential. As pastors, we have promised not to reveal the confessions of our members. In today's world many of those confessions may be made in a booth in a restaurant rather than one in the church, but they are still private. No story from the pulpit should cause a guessing game, "I wonder if he was talking about Hank and Jane?"

But stories about people in the congregation can make church members aware they are a part of the ministry of the church. Long ago I learned that I not only preach to people but also for them. (See chapter 10). Part of my job as a pastor of a congregation was to tell the stories of those people who shared their faith with me. Again, I'll give you some examples you may use, but the idea is to share the method, not just to give you another illustration.

1. In the last chapter about charts, I gave a sermon about grace and faith. This idea came from Bobby Carter in my confirmation class. I asked Bobby if I could use his idea and he was pleased. In the bulletin that Sunday a note

said: "The idea for today's sermon came from one of the confirmation students, Bobby Carter."

2. On a Monday morning, a member of the congregation called me to say she would have cancer surgery the next day. Before I could react, she continued, "I found out last Friday. It's major because it has to be taken out immediately. I was totally numb the rest of Friday and all day Saturday. I can't even remember what I did. I came to church only because that's what I do. I even forgot to put my name on the list of prayer requests. But when I received the Lord's Supper, a strange thing happened. I woke up! I realized I was ready for whatever happened. My faith has always been real—but I didn't know it was so practical." She asked me to tell her story—without her name.

3. As I studied a text from Ephesians, I realized I had a special insight on it because I had worked through several of the AA steps with one of our elders. I phoned him and asked permission to use what he had taught me. No one else would have asked where I had learned the point I wanted to share, but he would have, and I wanted to speak the message he gave to me to others.

4. Another AA story. One of our students brought a guest to confirmation class. The guest checked out the Bible and held up her hand. I went to her table. She pointed to several Bible verses and said, "This isn't fair! They stole this idea from AA." We had a great discussion before I explained when the New Testament was written and when AA started. I asked her if I could use her observation to help others see Christ in the AA program. I just did it.

5. I taught two elderly sisters in an adult instruction class. They asked if they could be baptized privately. I thought it was because they were shy, but one explained, "We don't want to criticize our parents. If two old ladies like us go up to be baptized, people will think our parents didn't do

right by us." I told them that I understood, but offered a deal. If they would be baptized in the worship service, I would tell the story to parents. They agreed. Did it again!

6. A confirmation student wanted to discuss (okay, she wanted to argue about) a Bible verse. We talked about it at length. Finally, she said, "Okay, I see what it means. But why didn't God just say it?" I answered, "Maybe he wanted us to talk about it so we would have to think for ourselves and learn from each other." I was surprised at the wisdom of my own answer. The two of us agreed that we should tell others what we had found together.

I am making myself stop the examples of stories from members of the congregation, though I suspect I have already included many such stories in other categories—and will continue to do so. We learn so much when we teach others and discover they have something to teach us.

Learn the history of your congregation from the old-timers. Many of them can tell stories that will help you understand the congregation—and are good illustrations for sermons.

1. When I was new in one congregation, an elderly gentleman explained, "It used to be that the pastor would come to a wedding reception, shake everyone's hand, and then leave. After that we would dance. We got this new pastor one time that stayed—just sat down and stayed. So we started to dance, and he scolded us. Don't you do that!"

2. On my third visit to a shut-in after I had been in a congregation for about six months, I realized she wasn't tuning in that day. I know my name is difficult; so I repeated the name of the congregation several times. "Oh," she said, "you're from the church. Tell me, how do you like that new pastor over there?"

When we use such stories, we are showing the congregation that we recognized they have been in Christian ministry long before we arrived. The pastor may be new, but the ministry is not.

One more way to use events from your congregation as illustrations in your sermons. Though they are not stories, a lot of classes, meetings, service projects, and other things happen in your church. We do all of these things because they are a part of the ministry of Jesus Christ. Sometimes we need to be reminded, and we need to remind the members of the congregation, that our church work is not just busy work; it is the work of Jesus Christ.

Therefore, when you come to the how-is-this-done part of the sermon, the place where you suggest action because of faith in Jesus Christ, point to the bulletin for the week. Emphasize the programs of the congregation directly related to the text. You can avoid making this into a commercial for parish programs by first identifying our need to service Christ. One of the joys of being a member of the body of Christ is knowing that no one person can do all the things Jesus asks us to do. We each do something. The text may tell us to help people in need. You can do that as an individual. You can do that by participating in the following activities in our congregation—show them in the bulletin or parish newsletter. You can do that through denominational agencies. In each case the church is needed to help the individual serve. This is also true of education, worship, fellowship, evangelism, stewardship, and other activities that are a part of a Christian life.

Don't limit the service of the individual member by the activities of the congregation. Also invite them to find other ways for the congregation to work together in ministry.

ETC.

There are many other sources of stories that make good sermon illustrations. A good rule of thumb is that the best stories are those you hear in the routine things of life. Current events provide such a wealth of stories that they will be treated in a separate chapter. Advertisements, movies, fantasy, *Reader's Digest*, are all a part of people's lives. The one who wants to be a storyteller must first be a story-listener. Listen well!

CHAPTER 7

How to Use Sound Bites, Phrases, and Words as Illustrations

Many people want to curse sound bites as the plague of modern communication. The sound bite and its sibling in the print media—the bumper sticker—have become the whipping boys for shallow thinking, deceit, and short attention spans.

However, the sound bite has been around a lot longer than one might imagine. In a previous generation the sound bite was known as a one-liner. The one-liner is a joke, put-down, or word of wisdom that can be condensed to one line. The TV program "Laugh In" changed the art of telling jokes into one-liners. The best of communication skills includes the ability to put a great thought into a one-liner. Graffiti—a highly influential form of written communication—is based on the ability to say it simply but to make it stick. Graffiti cannot be written in pages or paragraphs. Many times it communicates without using a full sentence.

The keep-it-simple method of communication also existed before the one-liner. It became a literary art form as a quote or an aphorism. Those words sound more profound—more worthy to be used in homiletical circles.

Words may be used to conceal—or to reveal. Words may confuse or enlighten. Words may be used to impress or to educate. Words may be used to fill space, like food with no calories. The words and phrases you use in a sermon may be little lights that twinkle to help people see your message. Or, they may be black holes in your sermon because your hearers do not know what you are talking about. Hearing a sermon with words one does not understand is like reading a page with words cut out by a censor. The remaining words lose their meaning also. Let me illustrate:

The cast for Redd Foxx's TV program "Sanford and Son" included two cops who worked in the local black community. One officer was black, the other white. The white cop would speak in official police language. He once told a crowd, "We apprehended the suspect with incriminating evidence upon his person." All of the people turned to the black cop, who interpreted, "They nabbed the dude with a joint in his pocket."

Your job is to speak the language the people in your pews use in their homes, schools, and on their jobs—with certain exceptions I trust you to avoid. Your message is to help people know Christ is with them in all parts of their lives. If you don't speak the Gospel so it reaches the everyday lives of your people, they get the idea the message about Christ is church talk. They may learn to use church talk with you on Sundays, but your message won't apply to Monday through Saturday. Your language shows your own understanding of life. Let me illustrate:

One of my fellow students in the seminary was from New York City. He thought our school was in a little town— though it had over 100,000 residents (a big city to me). He had a hard time dealing with life in the country—such as classes at 7:45 in the morning. I was alarmed when I heard he was assigned to a farm congregation in Iowa. Several years later I had a chance to see him in Iowa at a meeting of church leaders. He was at a table with members of his church. It was obvious they liked him and he liked them.

At a gathering in his home later, I could see why they liked him so much. He had been willing to learn from them.

They taught him about the farm, and he taught them about Jesus. The farmers enjoyed telling the story how they explained the difference between a sow and a gilt. In a human world the gilt would be a bride. The city pastor learned to use farm talk. He could even laugh at his city ways from the pulpit and ask for help in communication.

One more: Recently, I heard a professional theologian speak. His job description is to formulate church position papers. I admire him for telling about his seatmate on a recent flight—a woman who recently came to the U.S. from China. She asked him to explain the Christian religion. He said he suddenly realized his vocabulary was inadequate, though the woman understood English quite well. He was geared to speak to people with a theological education. Without saying it, he told us our job was to translate his language into that of our people.

As you plan your sermon, think of yourself sitting at a table with a group of people from your church. They are free to come and go as they please. Talk your sermon to them in a way that would make them want to stay to hear what you have to say. By sprinkling your message with meaningful and interesting quotes, phrases, and words you can keep the people at your table. Powerful words are like the chips in a chocolate chip cookie—they're what make it worthwhile.

SOUND BITES, ONE-LINERS, QUOTES

No matter what you call them, think of them as one-line illustrations. They can be used in all the ways other illustrations are used.

1. A quote is a good way to start a sermon. By definition, the quote has boiled a message down to a simple statement. It can help the people focus on the intent of the sermon. Sometimes, the quote might be from the text itself, "Jesus said ...," or "Paul said ..." By shining the spotlight on one thought of the text, you can tell the congregation what the focus of the sermon will be. Or, you

can use a quote from another part of the Scripture or another source. Luther said, "For where God built a church, there the Devil would also build a chapel." That could introduce a sermon that helps us Christians realize that the Devil hasn't given up on us yet.

2. A quote summarizing a sermon makes a good conclusion. For a sermon on the many texts that tell us not to try to guess when Christ will return to judge us: Luther said, "If I knew the world would end next Tuesday, I would still plant a tree today." (For the footnote fans among us: Everyone quotes the above from Luther, but I have never seen the original source.) A Bible verse is a good sound bite to end a sermon—perhaps the same one that was used in the introduction.

3. A brief quote can also be a good illustration to help the hearers remember a point. For a sermon on any of the times Jesus told us we must be like children, one point could be that all adults still have a child in them. The Gospel has to reach that child. William Wordsworth wrote, "The child is father of the man."

4. A variation of well-known phrases can catch the hearers' attention and give a message. A friend recently asked me, "If I say something in a forest and no one hears what I said, will I still be wrong?"

Think of a quote that you use as an illustration in a sermon as a small flashlight. A story, concept, or object lesson is a beacon—a major light. A beacon makes a bigger light and is more memorable, but there are times when you need a flashlight. A quote helps identify a smaller part of the sermon. Those who listen well will get and appreciate the quote. The less dedicated hearers may miss it, or not retain it. But that's okay. We need to learn that everything we say does not have to be filed in long-term memories.

WHO SAID IT?

It is important to know where the quote originated. Try this:

1. The captain of the Titanic said, "Do not be worried and upset. I am going to prepare a place for you."

2. Jesus said, "Do not be worried and upset. I am going to prepared a place for you" (John 14:1a, 2a).

The quote is exactly the same—the meaning very different. Sometimes the power of the quote comes from the one who originated it. This is true of Scripture. Sometimes people don't recognize the authority of a quote because we don't cite it. Let me illustrate:

I got cornered at a party once by another guest who wanted to tell me she had gone to a Bible college, and she was disappointed in the churches in our town because none of them preached the Bible. I invited her to the church where I was the pastor. She came. I phoned her the next week, and she said she appreciated that I had preached a message from the Bible. However, she would not come back because of something in our worship service that came from Luther—and she didn't agree with him. I asked her what it was. She said, "In your service you said, 'He that believes and is baptized shall be saved.' I know Luther said that, but I don't believe it." She wouldn't believe Jesus said it until I asked her to look up Mark 16:16. You guessed it. She didn't come back to church. If the quote had been cited in our order of worship, I would not have had to embarrass the biblical scholar.

Perhaps the idea of printing the words of Jesus in red would help. But when we speak, we need to identify sources from God's Word, if not by book, chapter, and verse, at least as from the Bible.

Some other quotes have value in themselves but have more if the source and context are included. For example:

1. "Crime is not traced to the lack of material things. It happens through loss of values." That quote would help

in any sermon on the First or Tenth Commandments. Fife Symington, then former governor of Arizona, said it. His family and his wife's family are wealthy. Later, he was charged with 21 counts of bank fraud, convicted of seven, and had a hung jury on 11. One could say he was a hypocrite to make the statement about values after he had already committed fraud, but had not yet been caught. I think not. I appreciate his statement because it has more value coming from him. He's been there. He was rich, but he wanted more. He recognized that his values were bad. If a poor person spoke that quote, it would be of less help to me because he wouldn't know the temptation of wealth. If a rich, honest man spoke those words, it might be boasting. But a rich crook can teach us a lesson about values.

2. "Being in the military I've moved around a lot and belonged to lots of congregations. I always get too involved or not involved enough. I can never get it right." The quote comes from Bill Benke. Only his family and friends would recognize his name. But many people will recognize his experience. Notice that he had always gotten involved in a congregation when he moved. He didn't even think about that as special. I do. He spoke with authority because he shared his experiences—not just his ideas. We who serve Christ never get it just right. His quote helped me as I retired and adjusted from the relentless schedule as a pastor to the freedom of writing when I want to.

Cite the source of a quote and/or give its historic background only when it will help the hearers get the message.

SOUND BITES AS THOUGHT PROVOKERS

Each of us will have our own favorite kind of illustrations and our favorite way of using them. The concern is for all of us to improve our communication of Christ's love and mercy. All of this is a way of saying quotes are not my favorite type of sermon illustration; though I sometimes use them. I know others who use them very effectively.

My favorite use of a quote is as a thought provoker. For me it works this way: If I present an idea, some people hear it as a conclusion. They seem to think their job is to agree or disagree. I think their job is to do some of their own thinking. If I use a quote without approving of it or disapproving of it, we can use it to think about an issue. The purpose is not to agree with or disagree with the quote, but to decide how we understand it and what we can get from it. Let me illustrate:

1. Voltaire said, "If God did not exist, it would be necessary to invent him." This quote can be heard in two very different ways:

   a. We cannot understand our own existence without understanding the existence of God. Therefore, if we do not know the God who created us, we have to invent one in order to explain who we are. Life makes no sense without God.

   b. People have invented the concept of a god to explain things they do not understand. God exists only in the human mind. Any god will do.

What do you hear in Voltaire's quote? Perhaps I limited the interpretation. Would the quote help you discuss your faith with an unbeliever? Does the fact that you know God through Jesus Christ give you a different slant on the quote?

2. Now for a less profound source: Two side-by-side billboards each had a public service message. They were:

   a. The Future Belongs to the Fit.

   b. Hire the Handicapped.

I'm sure I would never have remembered either one by itself, but together they grabbed my attention. I agree with the first. Take good care of yourself. Don't smoke! Eat your veggies! Exercise! Wear your seatbelt. I also agree with the second.

Those who have a handicap may have other high-level skills. Have compassion on those who need special help. Even those who caused their own handicaps live under Christ's grace and forgiveness. Let's help them make the best of it. The thought of each becomes more meaningful when we have to decide which one applies to the situation at hand. You can find two similar messages in Galatians 6. In verse 2, "Help carry one another's burdens." And in verse 5, "For everyone has to carry his own load." You are responsible to decide which message applies to the situation you are facing. Your faith in Christ makes you trustworthy to make your own decision.

3. Now let's go to what some people regard as the bottom of the communication chain: the bumper sticker. How do you understand the one that says, "Question Authority!"? Does it appeal to your sinful nature? Or, to your new nature in Christ? I like the message. As a Lutheran, I was taught that every once in a while someone has to nail some theses to the church door. As an American, I was taught that we have to throw a tea party now and then. Human authority always needs to be watched. Those who have authority should appreciate the suggestion: Question authority. It will help keep them honest. It shows people care. Those who must obey authority cannot use that as an excuse for doing wrong. They've got to check out the authority. However, the same message can be seen as attacking authority. To some, the bumper sticker is a call for rebellion and the destruction of all authority. Either way, the message gives us something to think about.

WHERE TO FIND YOUR SOUND BITES

Read.
Listen.
Your reading material will be one of your best sources of quotes to illustrate your sermons. A seminary professor told

our class that the problem with most sermons comes from the fact that the preacher reads too much theological and administrative material. He suggested we read at least one novel a month and several popular magazines. Check your reading habits. Do you read things you can quote in a sermon? Can you translate what you read to the language of your people? This suggestion does not implyyour church members are not educated people. Many may be more educated than we are, but in *specialized* areas. You couldn't understand their shoptalk, and they can't understand yours.

As I have worked on this chapter, I regret I did not use my *Familiar Quotations* by John Bartlett more. None of us have the time to go back and read all of the great literature of the ages. A book of quotes gives us the benefits of the thinking of many great people in the past. That is good for our own thought process. We also can pass wisdom from the past on to others. Let me illustrate:

We often quote, "O that we could see ourselves as others see us." Do you know that the quote comes from a church story? It is from Robert Burns' "Ode to a Louse." A man is sitting in church when a well-dressed lady, obviously with a high regard for herself, sits down in front of him. During the sermon, he notices a louse crawling in her hair.

I also like to watch for quotes I don't agree with. We never learn if we only read things we already know. A quote from the opposition can make us check our own sources and can help our hearers be armed to face other points of view. If you are speaking on a controversial subject, one that many members of the congregation may have a different point of view than you do, use a quote from the other side. Be fair about the quote. Those who disagree need to know you understand why some can have a different view. Then you can state why you have your view.

We also need to listen for quotes. In one of my little fantasies, I saw myself in heaven's library. I love books and the thought of a library with no limits on how long we can keep a book sounded like heaven to me. Then I realized we won't need books in heaven. Books contain the thoughts and feelings of people. In heaven we can go to the primary source—people themselves. We can do that here on earth too. We need books to get the wisdom and emotion of the past, but for the present, people will do it for us.

Sometimes I feel an important part of my ministry has been to listen to the wisdom of others and to pass it on. Maybe that's just in my job description, but you might be doing it to. You've gotten a lot of this passed-on-wisdom in other parts, but I need to tell you a few here.

1. I learned something about worship from a woman who started attending a church where I was the pastor. Her neighbor (who relayed the story to me) asked why she had chosen that church. She said, "I don't understand some of the things they do yet, but they let me do it with them."

2. A man and his 10-year-old son walked into church for the first time. (The member who sat behind them reported this.) I announced, "In the name of Christ I forgive all of your sins." The son asked his father, "Can he do that?" The father answered, "I don't know, but if he can, we've got the right place."

3. I had been traveling a lot and when I came home late one night, my wife said that our 10-year-old son had asked me to wake him up. I did. He told me that he missed me. With a little guilt, I told him I loved him even when I wasn't with him. He answered, "I know, but you can't hug a daydream."

4. When I was a small boy in the late 1930s, the farmer next to us was full of the anticommunist feelings that spread across our country. He talked about the "Reds" all the time. I saw the pictures of Russian armies in *Life* magazine and had dreams of them coming across our farm. One day, the neighbor said to my dad, "Harry, what would you do if the communists took over?" My father said, "I

guess I'd keep on farming." Then I knew my dad wasn't scared of the communists. The bad dreams went away.

5. I have often felt I am the exact opposite of a tel-evangelist. They cure everyone. When I called on people to ask why they hadn't been in church, most of them told me about their bad health. With one exception, Mildred Moore. Because of back problems, she was in permanent pain. On time, when I saw her dragging herself to church, I told her that if she stayed at home, I would bring the Lord's Supper to her. She replied, "Why stay home? It hurts just as bad there as it does here."

Listening for wisdom in daily life has given me a new slant on the question "If a tree falls in a forest and no one hears it, does it make any noise? My question is "If a wise thing is said and no one listens, is it still wisdom?" A lot of wisdom may have been lost because no one was listening.

PHRASES AS SERMON ILLUSTRATIONS

I am using a camera with a zoom lens. First we focused on a story, then on a sound bite (whatever), now on a phrase. A phrase is a group of words that pool their meanings to give a special thought.

A PHRASE AS A PARABLE

Many times a phrase becomes a miniparable. Paul talks about his "painful physical ailment" (2 Corinthians 12:7). In a literal sense Paul backed into a cactus and got a thorn in the flesh. We can understand that as a pain in whatever flesh we have in mind.

However, when you read the rest of chapter 12, it is obvious the messenger of Satan is more than a localized physical owie. This is a parable. Paul grew up with a Bible story about thorns—the same one we were taught and that we teach. When Adam and Eve sinned, God added thorns to many plants. Every thorn became a physical or visual reminder of our sinfulness. Paul's sin was a thorn in the flesh. The devil used the message in an effort to make him give up. But Paul knew God's grace in Jesus Christ was greater than all of his sin and of all the sin in the world. Jesus pulled the thorn out.

Watch for other phrases in the Bible that become mini-parables for us each time we hear them. My list is to help you watch for many more:

1. The valley of the shadow of death

2. Fishers of men

3. Daily bread

4. Built on a rock

5. Built on sand

6. Pearl of great price

7. A house divided against itself

Phrase parables need not all come from the Bible. We use many in our daily lives. Again, just to get you started:

1. A stitch in time

2. Time flies.

3. Apple of my eye (that one started in the Bible)

4. White elephant. This deserves an explanation. Centuries ago, in India, an albino elephant was regarded as sacred. People would neither work nor kill a white elephant. So if you had to give a gift to someone you didn't like, you gave him a white elephant. The new owner had to feed and provide for it but got no benefit from owning it. Hence, a white-elephant sale offers you something that will be worthless to you, but it might cost you to have it.

5. Black market

6. Domino theory

7. The eye of a storm

If you want to do more to study how words and phrases take on special meanings, I suggest *I Hear America Talking*,

An Illustrated History of American Words and Phrases, Stuart Berg Flexner (Simon and Schuster, 1976). Or, try a new version of the same idea (I've read reviews but not seen the Book) *Speaking Freely: A Guided Tour of American English from Plymouth Rock to Silicon Valley*, by Flexner and Anne H. Soukhanov (Oxford University Press).

PHRASES FOR ECONOMY OF WORDS

Phrases may also be used to communicate a big message in a short time. The combination of certain words increases the meaning of all of them and often creates a totally new meaning.

In a sermon I heard last week the pastor referred to a "God-sized opportunity." Voltaire talked about "the embarrassment of riches." Thomas Jefferson's "pursuit of happiness" still helps us distinguish between goals and means to a goal. Dietrich Bonhoeffer forced us to be more accurate when we use the word *grace* because he coined the phrase "cheap grace."

Those who write TV and radio ads have become masters at the economical use of words. Let them be your mentors. "Been there," "Done that," and "Where's the beef?" have worked their way into the language and literature of our country.

Many regions have special phrases that communicate well. In Arkansas those who are tense have their chain wrapped too tight on the axle. In Mississippi those who have achieved more than others in their family have risen above their raisings.

Each denomination (and perhaps each pastor) has developed many special phrases to give a shorthand message of an important idea. My denomination delights in Law and Gospel; faith alone, grace alone, and scripture alone; means of grace, and even third use of the Law. Some talk about deeds and creeds, born again, back sliding. All of those special phrases have been filled with meaning for those who understand them. However, it would be a good idea to occasionally take the time to redefine the often-used phrases for those who never learned, and for those who have forgotten, their spiritual significance.

All of us develop our own pet phrases that can be helpful in our communication to those who know us and know the meaning of our verbal shorthand. Some of these can become bad habits. I once knew a pastor who could not refer to the second person of the Trinity without saying, "Our Lord and Savior, Jesus Christ." His overuse of the phrase took away some of it's beauty.

Look for the Right Phrase

Look and listen for phrases that help you understand something better than you did before. As a pastor, you have an advantage most speakers don't have. You also have an opportunity to listen to the people who listen to you. I once asked a confirmation student what it means to renounce the devil, all his works, and all his ways. The student answered, "If the devil moves into my neighborhood, I've got to move out." His answer was more understandable than mine, so I've used it ever since. Avoid slang that is not age appropriate for you, or quote the phrase by saying, "as a teenager might say ..."

I was recently reading some children's sermons. One of them told me to "Hold up the bank." Sounds bad! However, it was a direction given for the person who was using the sermon to hold up the object being used, a piggy bank.

A Word as an Illustration

Our language would be dull and limited if every word had only one meaning. Most words have a variety of degrees, shades, and definitions. The speaker or writer has the responsibility to use a word so its meaning is clear to the hearer or reader. That's not easy. I already mentioned the time I used *story* to mean *narrative* and someone heard it to mean a lie. I will pass on two sad, but true, stories. The people who seem to be the villains in these stories are not stupid people. I tell the stories to show how easy it is for people to misunderstand a simple word because they think it has only one meaning.

1. A pastor right out of the seminary was called to a conservative congregation. He knew that some of the people suspected he didn't accept all of the miracles in the Bible. He decided to ease their minds by preaching on the story of Jonah on the second Sunday in his new parish. He told the story of Jonah and the big fish as a true story and applied it, as Jesus did, to the resurrection of Christ. The next week the congregation was abuzz with criticism of the pastor because he talked about the big fish rather than the whale. They said he really didn't believe the Bible. The word *whale* is used twice in the KJV, but never connected with Jonah. It is used once in the RSV (Matthew 12:40) and does refer to the story of Jonah. Though the pastor was correct in what he said, many in the congregation blamed him for their lack of knowledge.

2. A pastor had been in a congregation for about six months when an embarrassed circuit counselor told him an elder of the congregation had complained because the pastor did not preach the Gospel. The pastor could not believe anyone could say that of him. He was committed to a clear proclamation of Jesus Christ. As requested, he met with the elder and the circuit counselor. The elder said, "He never preaches the Gospel. He always preaches the Epistle."

Do not let these stories frighten you into silence. Instead, when you disagree with someone else, check for sure that you're getting the right meanings on the right words. Also, be aware that people will misunderstand what you say. Be accessible so they can tell you when they don't get it. You'll help them, and you may learn more about communication.

Words are our basic tools. The power of a word is not in its dictionary definition(s) but in its usage. Powerful words such as grace, mercy, and peace may be used in a repetitious, meaningless way. Or, a simple word may be given great power by how it is used. My wife and I recently had guests for a pasta dinner. She displayed two containers of Parmesan cheese and said, "This one is fat free, low salt, and no cholesterol. This one is …" As she paused to find the right word, I supplied it, "Good!" The word *good* is generally weak praise. In that case the guests understood and were able to make their choice by taste or by diet restrictions.

A Word as a Parable

Many words have both a literal and a symbolic meaning. In the dictionary, both meanings are listed to show the full use of the word. If the speaker wants to use the literal meaning but a hearer receives the symbolic meaning, the message is lost. The reverse is also true. Let me illustrate with a simple word. I'm going to use this word because the first story comes from an important part of my ministry and because it involves a number of issues in the Scriptures.

The word is *dog.*

No big problem. We all know what a dog is, but I had a lot to learn on the subject. My first call was to start a congregation in southern Mississippi. I met a farmer who also raised dogs, trained them to herd cattle, and sold them. He told me his mother objected to his sideline business because the Bible says, "Do not have the price of a dog in your house." He said he had asked several local pastors and all agreed that he should get out of the dog business, but none could find the passage. I assured him I thought he was in an honest business but I'd check for him.

I went to my concordance. It's there. Only it says, "Thou shall not bring the hire of a whore, or the price of a dog, into the house of the Lord thy God for any vow" (Deuteronomy 23:18 KJV). The fact that it refers to God's house, not ours, seemed to be of little help. But it did seem like a strange business combination to me. Wondering why they hadn't taught me things like this in the seminary, I checked a commentary. The word *dog* was used at that time to refer to a homosexual. The verse tells us not to use money gained by male or female prostitutes for our offerings to the Lord. I explained this to my farmer friend and told him he could tell his mother. He replied, "Never mind. I can live with it."

Most of today's translations have translated the word according to its symbolic meaning. The RSV still says dog, but a footnote explains it is a Sodomite. The NKJV also uses the literal translation. Some translations want to make the issue about temple prostitutes, male or female, but most just deal with the issue of prostitution.

Though I admit I used this subject as an excuse to tell that story, my point is that by limiting a word to one meaning, we can change the message of Scripture. The Deuteronomy passage has nothing to do with selling dogs to herd cows. On the other hand, if every person has the option of which of the acceptable definitions of a word is the proper one, we would lose the meaning of many other sections of God's Word. The rule for pastors is that we must use words according to their use in the Scriptures and, if there is cause for confusion, we need to explain what the text means to the best of our abilities. Always remember that the one who wrote the text put the meaning in the words. Our job is to know what the writer meant—not what we want it to say. In today's world, do not say that Paul got "stoned" in Lystra—or any place else.

We're not through with the word *dog* yet. Jesus tells a Gentile woman she cannot give the children's food to dogs (Matthew 15:26). He compares her to one below any human level, but as one in a high animal category. She accepts the title and asks for the rights of a dog. Jesus then tells her she is a woman of great faith. We understand Jesus said that she was like a dog. This is not quite a symbol, but it shows a wider use of the word.

In Philippians 3:2 Paul tells us, "Watch our for those who do evil things, those dogs, those men who insist on cutting the body." Is he warning us about dogs that might attack us when we make pastoral calls? Of course not! Most of the translations I checked stick with dog as the word used, and depend on us to understand it as a word for those who do evil and demand circumcision for Gentiles. CEV says, "those people who behave like dogs!"

Now for the last reference—the most difficult for those who work with children. Do you know the Bible says dogs will not go to heaven? After telling us about those in heaven, we read, "Outside are the dogs, those who practice magic arts, the sexually immoral, the murderers, the idolaters and everyone who loves and practices falsehood" (Revelation 22:15 NIV). Notice how different it sounds when you read the entire list rather than just the reference to dogs. Obviously, this is not talking about animals. I would never show this to a child who asks the ever-present question about pets in heaven. Only TEV translates the word as perverts. Apparently, these are taking their cue from Deuteronomy 23:18.

Let's look at another word as a miniparable. Simeon told Mary that a sword would pierce her heart. (See Luke 2:35.) We can be reasonably sure that Mary was never stabbed by a sword, but we know what Simeon said came true. As Mary saw her Son die on the cross, she felt the spear. This does not mean a metal blade also pierced her, but we feel the pain through the miniparable of a sword. Simeon could have told her she would suffer a lot and have great emotional pain, but he communicated a more meaningful message by using the word *sword*. We get the picture.

A cross was originally a Roman method used for capital punishment. When we say Jesus died on a cross, we are using the first definition of the word. But because the Son of God died on a cross and rose again, the word has a new meaning. When we sing "Lift High the Cross," we are not referring to torture and death, but to resurrection and victory. Jesus gave the word yet another meaning when he said, "[You] must forget [yourself], carry [your] cross, and follow me" (Matthew 16:24). He is not telling us to reinstate the Roman method of execution. Nor is he telling us to wear crosses as jewelry. He gave a special meaning to his cross because he took our sins on himself. Now that he has removed the barrier between God and us, we can forget ourselves. We've been taken care of. Now we can carry the burdens for others. Our cross is our willingness to take our self-imposed burdens and the burdens of others to Christ. Notice how the word has grown in meaning. Some might argue against the third meaning because only the holy Son of God can die on the cross to pay for sins. That's true. But because he did that for us, he has redeemed us back into God's service. We, who share Christ's victory on the cross, now can carry the message of the cross to others. Jesus could have told us we must forget ourselves and serve him by serving others. However, by using the word *cross*, he connects our service with his sacrifice. Bearing the cross is not a pity party. It is a part of a victory celebration.

Many other words in the Scriptures have special meanings because they are in Scripture, and a part of the history of God's interaction with people. Watch for the words that have power. Look for those that confront the issues of faith. You will find a lot of these words as you see the words of the Bible move to words of the hymn. Speak the language of the Scriptures, not by using old English or pronouncing God as though it had three syllables, but by using the words and images of God's Word.

We can also use other words as miniparables. A sermon in Philippians 2:5f can be about an attitude transplant. We all know about organ transplants. One who has a diseased organ needs a transplant from one who has a healthy organ. Our attitudes are diseased. Look who offers us a transplant.

Isaiah 9:6–7 is a birth announcement. Isaiah 40:3–5 is a part of today's "Keep Our Highways Beautiful" program. Anyone can volunteer to keep a section of the highway clean.

Isaiah 42:1–4 is a letter of recommendation for someone applying for the job as Messiah. Isaiah 43:1–28 is a "Dear Israel" letter from God that sounds like a "Dear John" letter from a lover—until you get to the very end. The invitation in Isaiah 55:1–11 needs an RSVP. Isaiah 62 includes a change of address card.

As you read the Scriptures, see how it always speaks to the lives of the people. In many ways we are the same, but in some ways we are different. How would Jesus have told the Parable of the Sower and the Seed to city people who don't even plant seeds in pots? "Fishers of men" was a great mission title for people who earned their living by fishing. To people today, fishing is a hobby, an expensive one. How would Jesus have told that story to computer programmers and factory workers? Some Bible translations/paraphrases, such as *The Message* and CEV, attempt to use modern words to explain a text. Often they translate an idea rather than a word. By using a number of translations you will get both the translation of the word and the idea.

The idea of translating not just the words of the Bible, but also the ideas, is not new. The following is from a sermon preached by Francisco Davila in Quechua, Peru, in 1646:

> I am the good shepherd of the llamas, the shepherd with a great heart. For his llamas he has no fear of death. The shepherd who receives wages, and whose animals, like llamas, do not belong to him, when he sees a puma leaping, flees and runs away as fast as he can. The puma seizes a llama and scatters the others. And that is because the shepherd receives wages because the animals are not his. I am the good shepherd who knows his animals, and the animals also know me.
>
> But if he is the shepherd, who and what are his llamas, his animals? We are, and we alone. All human beings, men and women, are the llamas of Jesus Christ.
>
> *(Comby, Jean.* How to Read Church History, *vol. 2. London, SCM Press Ltd, page 73)*

Words for Three Dimensional Hearing

Years ago I said when I retired, I wanted to write the instructions for assembling children's toys and household appliances. Over the years I added to the list: all insurance policies, prospectuses for investments, all legal documents, and finally some theological statements. All of those things seemed to be flat English. They are dull, hard to follow, and totally forgettable.

I am retired, and I am not doing that kind of writing because I learned something. Many things must be written in precise, uninteresting ways. Many words are written but are not meant to be good reading. Some are written to protect the writer and/or the company. In a football world, they play on the defense. Boring is good because it allows for no mistakes and no misunderstanding. Never mind that it also may not give an understanding either.

In a football world, those who preach are playing for the offense. We speak for Jesus Christ who came into the world, not to defend the *status quo*, but to change it. That change is a continuing process that will not end until we hear a trumpet blast coming from angels.

Flat language becomes multidimensional when we use words that challenge us to think. A word that has a variety of possible applications makes the hearer responsible for understanding. The word doesn't stand by itself, but is a part of the other words in its neighborhood. If we are afraid that we might be misunderstood, we become too cautious and join the defense team. We teach a message of faith, and we need to proclaim that faith to those who hear us. Instead of using only the safe words that keep us inside the fort, we need to reach out to the world with a message that is sure—and the sureness is in Jesus Christ who came to the world.

I am going to suggest two ways of thinking about words to help gain two or more dimensions in verbal communication.

THE LOWLY PUN

A pun is a play on words that sound alike, but have different meanings. Even those who groan at every pun recognize they are a good way to make people listen carefully. Only those who think can understand puns. Most puns don't translate to other languages well. That's why we have missed a great pun from Jesus.

When our Lord was talking to Nicodemus (John 3), he talks about being born again—this time, of the Spirit. Nicodemus didn't get it. Jesus says, "The wind blows whenever it wishes; you hear the sound it makes, but you do not know where it comes from or where it going. It is like that with everyone who is born of the Spirit" (John 3:8 NIV). When the word *wind* is used in other parts of the New Testament, the Greek word is *anemos,* except for twice in Acts in this conversation. Here the word is *pneuma,* which means both wind and spirit. Jesus used the word *pneuma* as a pun. The double meaning of the Greek word helps us understand the work of the Holy Spirit.

Philip Melanchthon, whom few people would accuse of being witty, could not avoid a pun when he wrote about the papal degree that required all priests to become celibate, though priests had previously been allowed to marry. Some priests who refused to divorce their wives were hanged. Melanchthon commented that the pope said they should be suspended, but he meant from their office, not from a tree.

I am not suggesting that puns be used as jokes in a sermon. I am suggesting that when you are aware of the various meanings of words and the sounds of words, you can put an extra twinkle light into your sermons.

1. The bumper sticker said: JESUS SAVES! Someone asked, "At which bank?"

2. An elder offered his pastor a case of peach brandy if the pastor thanked him for the gift in the Sunday bulletin. The pastor accepted. The next bulletin said, "The pastor

thanks Mr. Schmidt for the gift of fruit and the spirit in which it was given."

3. During hunting season try, "Pray for the prey."

4. The pastor said, "You have sinned badly." One member commented, "Well, I did as well as I could."

5. True story: A missionary preaching through a translator said, "You must drown the old man that is in you." One lady later said, "You can drown my old man any time you want."

6. Bumper sticker: SAVED BY THE BLOOD OF CHRIST. Comment: What if he doesn't match my blood type?

7. Sunday school teacher, "And they [shepherds] came with haste, and found Mary, and Joseph, and the babe lying in a manger" (Luke 2:16 KJV). A student asked, "Wasn't it awful crowded in that manger?"

8. When I received a call to a congregation in Arizona, one of the teachers in my school said I could go if I wanted to be saved. I thought this was going to be a bad joke about Arizona's heat as compared to hell's. The teacher explained that as a child she had understood a Bible verse to say, "And he [Christ] is the propitiation for our sins: and not for [Arizona] but also for the sins of the whole world" (1 John 2:2 KJV; *Arizona* mistaken for "our's only").

These stories, and the many that you have heard, can be used to help people understand the meaning of words in the Scriptures. They can introduce a feeling of humor to prepare people for a heavy message to follow.

If you think puns are a low brow form of communication, listen to Louis Rukeyser on "Wall Street in Review" and Gene Shalet do movie reviews on "The Today Show." Both speakers have lifted puns to a high level method of communication.

OXYMORA

An oxymoron is a combination of words that does not make sense. In your mind, picture a round square. Try seeing a tall dwarf. I'd like to see a bonsai redwood tree. The devil's pitchfork is a well-known visual oxymoron.

As you see the devil's pitchfork, your eyes have to make a decision. Do you want to see three prongs or four? Both can't be true; though both can be seen. Verbal oxymora give you the same option.

Many oxymora that we use for humor today are not truly words that contradict one another, but are words that rub against one another. Tight slacks sounds like an oxymoron if you think *slack* has only one meaning. However, when you realize that slacks also means pants you also recognize that a lot of tight pants are parading around regularly. Jumbo shrimp is an oxymoron only for those who see shrimp as something small. Shrimp, as seafood, can be jumbo. Here's a favorite from one of my city-reared sons when we would go to the farm to pick berries. He told his brothers, "Red blackberries are green." His three-way oxymoron included one color, one plant title, and one condition of ripeness. When my first book was published, my children were unimpressed. They read them—why shouldn't I write them? One evening at dinner, I announced I had received my first royalty check. One asked, "What's that?" Another replied, "That's when they check your blood to see if it's blue." I began to wonder who should be writing books around that house. Oxymora provide a way to use words that attract attention, require thinking, and spice things up a bit. They add a twinkle to a sermon.

I was jogging early one morning and went past a drug store in a shopping center. There were two signs on the door. One said: OPEN. The other said: CLOSED. Obviously, only one sign could be correct. Wrong! Both signs were correct. The store was in a new shopping center and was one of the few stores that had been opened. The sign that said OPEN was correct. However, it was 6:00 A.M. and the store had not yet opened for business that day. The sign that said CLOSED was correct. Words must be read and heard in their correct context.

One more: Few people know what could be my greatest claim to fame. I was once Dick Gephardt's running mate. That statement is literally true and perhaps should be left as it stands. But the rest of the story is that we used to jog in the same park—and once in a while we jogged together.

More important, however, is the fact that the Scriptures have many oxymoronic phrases and concepts. Using these ideas as words in conflict helps us teach the message of many texts. Let me illustrate:

1. Jesus the God-Man is perhaps the greatest of all oxymora. Those who believe in one God already have accepted the fact that many gods is a true oxymoron. God is God. Men may try to replace God. They may make up other gods, but they can't be God. Yet Jesus who is God became a human being. The two words clash as well they should. The miracle of divine intervention in humanity is moronic by human reasoning, because it goes beyond our limitation—which is exactly what God has in mind. We don't explain or ease the tension between the concept of God and man in one person; rather, we glory in it.

2. The idea of a transcendental local God is also an oxymoron. God either needs to be up there, or down here. Which is it? The answer is yes. Yes, he is up there. Yes, he is with us, right here. Moronic, perhaps, to those who need to control things, but a source of joy and comfort for those who have faith in God who is both in control and who cares.

3. Sinner-saint is an oxymoron we will never fully understand. We who are (not were) sinners are saints now. We who are saints are also sinners. The ideas are in conflict. A great part of religious thought, including that of some Christians, is to find the dividing line between the sinner and the saint. Yet the Scripture addresses us by both titles. How can that be? Check God's Word.

4. Jesus gives us a chunk of bread and tells us to eat his body. He offers a cup of wine and tells us to drink his blood. Moronic? It is, to some. Others try to work out an understanding like I did with tight slacks and jumbo shrimp above. But others, including me, find great joy in the oxymoron of bread-body and blood-wine.

Search the Scripture to find the oxymora of faith. Don't take away the tensions that must exist if one is to deal with God and people in the same paragraph. Sure, we don't understand all of the ideas that seem to be contradictory from a human point of view. But that shouldn't surprise us. God has revealed himself through Christ so we can see him in our lives. Following Christ in faith leads us beyond what we can see and understand.

Many sermons can be based on the clash of human and divine thought. This struggle can be seen in the great scope of Christian history, and it can be seen in the struggle in each Christian as the sinful nature and the new nature in Christ war against one another. I suggest some sermons based on oxymora:

1. I work as an engineer, I serve Jesus Christ.

2. Our average life span is 75 years. We live forever.

3. I can commit adultery in my heart while I sing, "My Faith Looks Trustingly."

4. (The following was used as an offering prayer by a guest pastor at a congregation that I served.) Lord, this isn't all that we have, but it's all we're going to give today.

5. God speaks to me through the Bible. I read some of it last month.

6. "I do believe; help me overcome my unbelief!" (Mark 9:24 NIV)

Find your own oxymora in your life and the lives of the people around you. They are the evidence of the clash between us and the God-in-us. That is a good target for your sermons.

OLD WORDS—NEW MEANINGS

One reason we need frequent revisions of Bible translations is that words that remain the same may change meanings. Be careful when you read such words as suffer, stone (the verb), ass, and others from older translations. Many people will hear something that has no connection with the original word in the Scriptures. Notice how even our present day words change. We still talk about ice cubes, but they are no longer cubes. We dial phones that have no dials. Many hotels give you a key that looks like a credit card. Watch for the subtle changes in the meanings and usage of words. Watch for new words that express old thoughts. We can hope that *bummer* moves rapidly from slang to acceptability because it expresses an idea usually said in forbidden words.

PLAY WITH WORDS

I recognize that the subject of this chapter might not be regarded as sermon illustrations by some. When you use sound bites, phrases, and words as illustrations, your hearers will not identify them in the same way as they do a story or object lesson. But I am convinced that our ability to use word pictures and three-dimensional language gives power to a sermon. We spend a lot of time working on sermons. That effort should include time to play with words. I suggest the following:

1 Read authors who use words with flair and make simple words powerful. I hesitate to give you my list, but I will name a few who have helped me: John Updike, Garrison Keillor, Erma Bombeck, Dave Barry, and way back in history, Adlai Stevenson.

2. Work crossword puzzles—not the kind that asks for an Indian weight or a tree in South America. Look for the ones that make you think about words. I like the clues that give two words that are used with another, such as: *A six-letter word with Roman and Advent.* The answer is

candle. Or, the ones that make you think of a variety of meanings: *A four-letter word for Rent.* Lease won't fit. The first letter is T, so hire won't do. The answer: Tear.

3. Read books on the use of words.

4. Play word games. Example: use the names of animals as verbs to see how the meaning is changed. To make the noun a verb you will sometimes have to add a preposition, such as horse around or monkey with.

5. Check out anything by Richard Lederer. The man doesn't know when to stop.

6. Listen to conversations. Church council meetings are often not memorable events, but I recall one from 37 years ago. Someone said, "I have an idea I'd like to throw up."

7. Learn sign language for key biblical and theological words. Often the signs are good illustrations of the meaning of the words.

"A word fitly spoken is like apples of gold in pictures of silver" (Proverbs 25:11 KJV).

"The right word at the right time is like a custom-made piece of jewelry" (Proverbs 25:11, The Message).

CHAPTER 8

How to Use the Daily News as Illustrations

The message we preach is a part of the daily news. We preach from a book that starts with the first great news headline: GOD CREATES HEAVEN AND EARTH. We broadcast the news that God's Son became a human being, and that he died on a cross and arose again. These things could be studied as history, because from one point of view they happened a long time ago. But from our point of view, they started a long time ago, and today's sermon tells the latest doings of the God who created everything and of his Son who is the Savior of all. Our sermons are about the people that he created. We speak both to and about the people Christ has saved. Our message is not merely Good History. It is Good News.

As you watch a newscast, think about the God who introduced himself "in the beginning" and see him also present after, "Now for today's news." Listen to the international news and be aware that God is there where some people are fighting, some are hungry, and others are suffering from the storms of nature. Listen to the national news and remember that Jesus told us to pay the government what we owe. (See Matthew 22:21.) Paul told his readers to obey political leaders and to pay their taxes. (See Romans 13:1–6.) Those early Christians had to obey dictators. We need to obey and support those whom we elected. Does that make it easier or more difficult? It does make us more responsible. We need to teach that responsibility in our sermons and in our lives.

Give attention to the local news and hear Christ tell you to love your neighbor as yourself. In New Testament times most people would have known only a few hundred people. We know thousands and are aware of many more. The media has put a larger responsibility on us by making us aware of more neighbors. We also have more resources and more ways to help our neighbors. Some people avoid the news to avoid their responsibilities. We who believe in Christ and proclaim his message must help others see the people Christ loves.

Jesus used local news events to help people understand his message. Some people thought God punished each individual according to the sin of the day. They judged other people by the good or bad things that happened to them. Jesus pointed to two current events, Pilate killing some Galileans and a tower in Siloam that fell and killed 18 people, to show that those people did not die because they were more guilty than others. (See Luke 13:1–5.)

The news reports on all media zoom down from international to local events. Our newscast in a sermon goes two steps further. We can say, "Now for the latest news in our families." Then when we start a section, "Now for the news of each individual." The Good News of Jesus Christ reaches to all people and to each person.

AND NOW FOR THE NEWS

In previous chapters, I often had an urge to include an illustration from the news of that day. But I knew that by the time this book is published, sold, and read, that day's news will be history. For this section I'm going to forget that problem and use some recent news items. Since news headlines often seem to be recycled (that is, history repeats itself), you may be able to use some of these illustrations by connecting them with what's going on in the world on the day you preach. Also, some of these events have lasting value as sermon illustrations because the people involved will continue to affect events. But even more important, I want to encourage you to keep alert to current events and use news as illustrations in your sermons.

After I had been preaching for over 10 years, I got into one of those I've-got-to-do-better moods. I decided to go back through all my old sermons. I saw a lot of things that needed improvement—many of which are included in this book. But one of the things that surprised and encouraged me about my old sermons was the frequent use of the news of the day. Going through the sermons was like reading *Time* and *Newsweek* in the doctor's office. It was a good review of recent history.

Now for the news at the time I am working on this manuscript.

1. The death of Princess Diana has been the big news item for two months and probably will be the top news story for 1997. There are numerous sermon illustrations in the story from, "Wear your seat belts," "Don't ride with a drunk driver," to the issues of the rights of privacy for public figures. I saw one message in the news of her death that I want to share. Immediately after she was killed, the news was filled with stories of her great contributions to the world. She was proclaimed to be Queen of our hearts, and ambassador to the world without portfolio. Then a few reports told of her dark side. She had been unfaithful to an unfaithful husband. She wasted money. She neglected her children. As time goes on, more news accounts report the bad news about Princess Di. One panel of news people had a lively debate about which was the real Princess Diana. I wanted to get on the panel and say that both were the real woman. Do we have to be perfect to do anything good? Do the bad parts of our lives wipe out the good? Our Christian faith tells us we are sinner-saints. Our good deeds are not

destroyed by our sin. Our sin does not keep us from loving and serving God and others. We destroy the example of the good the Princess did if we make her a perfect person. We ignore the good she did if we want to dig out and listen to all of the dirt that may be true.

2. Another sermon illustration about Princess Diana's funeral, held in Westminster Abbey. Speakers and screens were set up outside the Abbey for those who were not formally invited to attend the funeral. In response to a song and to the words of the Princess' brother, the crowd on the outside applauded. Gradually the applause entered the rear of the church and spread forward to include all people. But the applause started in the parking lot and came into the church. The church believes Jesus Christ died for all people and he is risen from the dead. With a message like that, should not the applause start on the inside and spread to the world?

3. Mother Teresa died the same week Princess Diana was killed. Again, her life and death are filled with sermon illustrations—including the amount of news coverage given to her life and funeral as compared to that given to Diana Spencer Windsor. But I learned a great lesson from the Catholic nun. Her commitment to the poverty stricken people of India was beyond my ability to understand. She gave herself in a way I am not able to do. When I read about her work, I understood why. She did not think it was her mission to get rid of poverty in India. She was there to help those who needed food and medical care. She gave help to people rather than crusade about issues. She didn't measure her work by the problems she solved, but by the people she helped. I need that understanding. I think others need to understand the call Christ has given us to love people. We are not here to solve social and political issues. Jesus did not solve the problems of his nation during his time on earth. But he gave us a way to have God's help in those

problems, and he gives us a way to help one another. Our goal is to help people in need, to feed the hungry who will get hungry again, to forgive the sinners who will sin again. Change does happen, but it happens only because people have been helped.

4. Four more Mother Teresa stories must be included:

a. An American supporter visited her in India and went with her on her rounds to help sick people. As she led him toward a filthy hut filled with sick people, he said, "I wouldn't go in there for a million dollars." Mother Teresa replied, "Neither would I, but I'll do it for Jesus."

b. A Mother Teresa quote, "If you want to make God laugh, tell him your plans." A bonus point on quoting sources: After I had included the above line from Mother Teresa, I discovered it is also used in the play *A Letter of Resignation* by Edward Fox. It's a good line, no matter who originated it.

c. As a part of my work on this book I visited one or two churches, in addition to the congregation where I am a member, each weekend. On the Sunday after Mother Teresa's death I happened to be at a Catholic church. In the announcements the priest said, "Mother Teresa died this week. Now she's in heaven telling God what to do."

5. In the last few weeks there have been two airplane crashes that killed a large number of people, two strong hurricanes in the Pacific, and the constant threat of destruction from a volcano in the Caribbean. These tragedies are always big news events because they involve the lives of many people. If we have been in the area of destruction, or if we know people there, we pay special attention. We need to remember the people who are killed, injured, or lose homes and property in such events. But the lessons learned from the forces of destruction go beyond the event itself. Everyday, people die one by one from accidents and violence. Everyday,

someone's home burns down, a child plays with a gun and kills someone, a young mother dies of cancer, and a person is killed by a drunk driver. These events are reported only in the local news, if at all. The big events may get our attention and become illustrations of the needs of people all around us.

6. Last week, *Newsweek* had an article on the Pope's effort to have Mary given the title of co-redeemer. Also last week, *Time*'s cover story was on the expansion of Buddhism in the United States especially through the entertainment industry. People read these stories. They expect their church to help them understand how such distant events affect them today and what it means for the future.

7. The Promise Keepers gathered on the mall in Washington, D.C., and on every newscast across the country. We heard statements about sin and grace, about the Bible and worship, and about prayer in repentance on all the news programs. Most of the message was in the language we speak and often hear in church. But it sounded different on TV along with commercials, weather forecasts, and the stock market report. Do you want to join those who mocked the faith of the Promise Keepers? Or, do you want to use their message on TV as a way to speak your own faith?

8. The voters in California recently approved a referendum that denies illegal aliens (mostly from Mexico) rights to certain medical, educational, and other social programs funded by the state. That same referendum is being considered in other states. People have strong legal and humane arguments on both sides of the issue. I think if we asked Jesus about the subject, he would take out a dollar bill and ask whose picture is on it. Washington is the answer. And Jesus' response, "Give to Washington that which is Washington's and to God that which is God." That doesn't tell you how to vote on the referen-

dum about illegal aliens. But it does give you a way to think about the issue. As a citizen I see why we cannot pay for the needs of everyone who comes to our country. But as a Christian, I don't see any national or racial borders to divide people. When I give to Washington, I am helping Americans. When I give to God, I am helping people—God's people.

9. The birth of septuplets in Iowa received a lot of news coverage and a lot of editorial comments ranging from "What a great miracle from God" to "What an abuse of scientific advancements." It seemed as though people wanted to choose up sides for and against the family that had increased 233 percent in one day. Maybe that's the purpose of editorial pages and programs. We can gain understanding by knowing the opinions of others. However, the Scriptures make it perfectly clear God has not named us to be one of his judges. Jesus will take care of the judging. Thank God for that. We know when God tells us not to judge others, we are not to condemn them for their faults. Instead, we are to tell them of Christ's grace. The fact that we are not to judge others also has another important implication for us. Not only are we not to condemn, but also we do not have to approve of others in order to love them and help them. Our relationship with others is not based on right and wrong. I don't have to cheer or boo the parents of the seven womb mates born in Iowa. But I can love them and pray for them. I can be glad for the seven lives entrusted to their care.

Let me assign you to the news desk of your local newspaper or TV station. Your job is to read Psalms and Proverbs each day to find references that speak to news events of the day. You'll be surprised to find that the psalm writers and Solomon seem to be waiting for the anchor to say; "Now we go to the Bible for a word about today's news."

What Is Your News Source?

Sometimes you may be tempted to avoid all references to news events because news itself is a controversial subject. Many pastors avoided talking about the peace marches during the Vietnam era, the race riots, and bombing of abortion clinics even though those events were on the minds of all people. Christians also needed God's Word of Law and Gospel applied to such issues.

Or, you might be tempted to the opposite side by making yourself into a news commentator who gives the right view of all the news. I know of a pastor who, about 20 years ago, distributed an off-the-wall newsletter that identified communists. His list included Queen Elizabeth, almost anyone who supported the United Nations, and other assorted political leaders. He was asked to leave the congregation.

News is in itself a news item. The source of news is a problem for many people. Some see the news media as a monolithic unit with all people marching to the same beat. They see the news as either the left-wing, liberal press, or the right-wing, anger-driven talk radio shows. Perhaps those two extreme views help us understand the public press is not a controlled group. You can find news publications and programs that present every possible political view. It is strange to hear someone on the media denounce the media because it never allows a certain news item to be aired. If that were true, the critic would not have a camera and/or microphone available.

I mention this because we in the church should understand the problem. Some people often see us as a monolithic institution all under the control of someone other than the Holy Spirit. One televangelist cheats poor people out of their life savings and the whole church is guilty. One clergy is found guilty of molesting a child and all clergy are suspect. We know those generalizations are not fair. We also know that attacks on the news people should be on the one that has the byline, not on the news institution.

In order to use news events for sermon illustrations, we need to teach our people how to read or listen to the news. Do this by example, not by a sermon on the subject; though the first illustration below could become a sermon.

1. When Paul arrived in many cities, the people refused to hear his message. They were closed-minded; that is, their minds were like concrete—all mixed up and permanently set. However, the people in Berea (Acts 17:10–15) were open-minded. They listened to Paul, but they were not gullible. They checked Paul's message out by reading the Scriptures. The Bereans show us how we should listen to the news today. Don't be afraid to listen to someone who might be wrong; the person might be right. You could miss an important message (such as the way of salvation through Jesus Christ) by shutting out any new idea. On the other hand, don't let your mind be filled with junk. Use the Scriptures as a screen over your open mind.

2. All newscasters, as well as all clergy, are biased. They are people and each person has his or her own point of view, depending upon his or her experiences. Those who listen to the news are also biased. If the newsperson and you have the same bias, you will think the news is right on target. If you have a different bias, you will assume the news is wrong. You might be right, but it could be that your bias is wrong. Many news publications and individuals will identify their biases. They tell you why they think the way they do. That helps you also understand why you think the way you do. A Pentecostal church publication gave a positive review to my first book of children's sermon. The last line said, "We encourage you to use these sermons; however, remember they are written with a Lutheran bias." I was upset. How dare they say I had a bias! Then I realized that of course I had a bias. I should have. This book is also written with a Lutheran bias; though I hope other Christians can use it. The cross of Jesus Christ can bring their bias and my bias together.

3. People should know the difference between news items and editorial opinions. Those in the news media should help make the distinction. A news item tells you the facts, even though there may be sources that disagree with one another, and the reporter chooses which facts to include and which ones to omit. The editorial writers give their opinions. You may agree or disagree with the opinion. The idea is not to tell you how to think but to give you one person's view to help you look at the facts in that light. Many publications and programs match opposing but responsible editorial views to help the readers/listeners see at least two points of view. In our sermons we follow the same idea. When we say, "God says," we want to make sure that we correctly quote God—not just his words but also his meaning—in the correct context. When we say, "I think," we are giving our opinion and inviting others to think also.

4. Don't blame the media for giving us the bad news. Even we who proclaim the Good News of Jesus Christ also teach a message of Law and judgment. However, our Good News overrides the bad news of the Law. The world has a natural law, but there is no Gospel in nature or of human sources. Some have started publications to print only the good news of the world. All of them fail fast, but the good things should not be news. It is not news that I didn't kill anyone and I haven't robbed a bank. That shouldn't be news because it's the way things ought to be. Most of the news of the world is about things that aren't the way they ought to be. All news programs give us a scene of the Law on which we can project the light of the Gospel.

5. We, and those who hear us, need to be secure in an insecure world. Many read all of the evil of the world and become afraid. Jesus said, "Heaven and earth will pass away, but my words will never pass away" (Matthew 24:35 NIV). We can see the dangers of the world from the

safety of the Gospel. Watch for those who show panic and anxieties because they think society is going to hell in a handcart. Don't deny the problems of the world. Rather, put them under the victory that Christ has given us.

6. Recognize how much you are influenced by your sources of news. There are two extremes. You can read and listen to only those with whom you already agree will increase your security. There are times when you need that. But at other times it keeps you from learning new good things and from facing problems that need your Christian attention. If you read only those contrary to your faith, you may be pulled away from the truth of the Gospel. Examine yourself and ask which extreme you are nearer. Listen to those who listen to your sermons and find out what news sources are influencing them. A woman in my parish was always angry about the church and always quoted from a bad-news-Christian source. I told her that she would be a better Christian and a happier person if she read more of John's gospel and less of the yellow church journalism. She became even angrier at my suggestion. However, six months later she told me she had followed my suggestion, and it worked.

There was a time, as when I grew up, that the pastors were the only or the most educated people in the congregation. They were, or were assumed to be, the authorities on all things. The church was the chief source of information for most people. I learned the Japanese had bombed Pearl Harbor at a Sunday evening church service. But it's not that way any more. The people who attend church are influenced by many sources. They are overwhelmed by information. We do not want to use the church as a place to hide from reality. We who preach need to be aware of the sources of news and other information used by those who also use us as a source. We do not compete with the other communicators. We do not have to prove they are wrong and we are right. It is our task to add the Gospel of Christ to the message of the world.

News Is an Emotional Issue

While we often think of the news as objective fact, it is actually an emotional experience to listen to the news. Some people yell at the news crew on TV. Some tear up magazines and newspapers to show their disagreement. Some cancel subscriptions or click the remote control button. Others get a daily fix of greed from the financial pages, a daily fix of anger from editorials and talk radio, or a fix on sexual lust from tabloids and pseudonewscasts. The news offers us heroes and villains. Listening to the news can make us feel guilty or self-righteous.

We who preach need to be aware of emotional reactions to news events so we do not fan the fires of greed, prejudice, lust, and anger. We need to use the Law to help people understand their reactions to news. It can be one way to help people recognize themselves. You might try variations of some of the following questions, written as though they are addressed to you the preacher. You must first deal with your own political views and apply your faith in Christ to the issues. Then you can use the same questions, and the same faith, to help those who hear you apply their faith to the same issues.

1. When the team you support wins, do you feel you have won? What have you done to contribute to that victory? What have you gained from that victory? Could you use the elation you feel about your favorite team's win as a way to understand your joy of Christ's victory over death? Could you cheer for those who are working to share the love of Christ in words and actions with the world? Is the comparison between the victory of a team and of Christ over death fair? Does Christ's victory have more to do with your life than the team's victory?

2. When your favorite team loses, do you feel you have lost? If so, what have you lost? Do you get angry with those who support the team that defeated your team? Do you agree with the concept "The enemy of my

enemy is my friend" in the realm of sports? How much of your security is built on the win-lose ratio of some sport? Do you pray more for victory in the sports arena than the victory of the Gospel in the world arena? What would change your priorities?

3. Do you get angry when discussing political views with someone who disagrees with you? Do you think our country (state or local community) would be better off if everyone voted for the same political party or candidate that you do? Would you accept the responsibility of casting a tie vote for all political races—which means your name would be in the paper as the one who chose the winner?

4. Do you believe God belongs to the same political party that you do? Can you understand that sincere Christians can vote for opposing candidates? Using political illustrations can be hazardous to your spiritual message, but since this book is about illustrations, I am going to take the risk. During the 1996 campaign I had a phone message to call an 800 number to speak to Speaker of the House Newt Gingrich's office. Since I had a fun-loving staff, I assumed the number would reach Dial-a-Prayer. However, the person who answered said he was from the Speaker's office—not Mr. Gingrich. In the conversation, he told me no Christian could vote for a Democrat. Would someone else have said no Christian could vote for a Republican? The purpose of our two-party system is not to control us, but to give us an opportunity to express our own priorities in the ballot box. My priorities include my Christian faith. I believe we should encourage all Christians to express their faith. The difficulty is that we may agree with one party or candidate on one moral subject, but with the other side on another subject. That's why we need a lot of people voting.

5. Pick a political leader you support. Do you agree with every political opinion the person has? Does that mean

you must also agree with every action of that person? Try naming one thing your favorite politician has said you disagree with. Another illustration that may involve a risk. Here I am setting an example for you about being fair. My previous illustration might be seen as anti-Republican. The next might be regarded as anti-Democrat. A friend's mother was a pious Catholic. She was overjoyed when Senator John Kennedy became President John Kennedy. She applauded everything that he said and did. A stray Republican in her family pointed out some of Kennedy's sexual escapades. The conflict between her piety and her political feelings clashed. She finally made a choice and said, "He works very hard, and he needs some way to relax."

6. Now focus on a politician you can't stand. Certain political figures attract both deep loyalty and deep resentment. Many people loved to hate President and Mrs. Reagan. Now many other people love to hate President and Mrs. Clinton. (There's a well-balanced political illustration.) If you fall into either category, can you name something good about the couple you love(d) to hate?

I have used sports and politics as examples of emotive issues on the news, there are many others. The tabloid newspapers, talk shows on radio and TV, and many specialized magazines all have a big influence on the way people think. Many people deny that they read, hear, or watch such news sources. When they want to tell a story from such, they most often introduce it by saying: "I never watch that program, but I had the TV on while I was waiting for the news," or "I don't read that publication, but I saw it as I was in the grocery line." However, such publications and broadcasts have a big influence on people—including those who go to church.

Church news is also an emotional issue. We often complain because the Christian faith and Christian people are attacked by some in the media. Last evening's news told about an attempt to teach the Bible in an elective high school class in Florida. One condition required that it not include the resurrection of Christ. To a Christian, that would make as much sense as a sports story that didn't tell who won.

As Christians, however, we must also recognize that a lot of the religious news is about Christians trashing other Christians. Notice how often people use Christ and the Bible to promote violence, prejudice, and divisions. Are our sermons part of the problem or a part of the solution?

Let's look for some guidelines on ways we can speak about news events to help people live their faith rather than add to the problems of anger and divisions.

1. Do not use harmful words, but only helpful words, the kind that build up and provide what is needed, so that what you say will do good to those who hear you. (Ephesians 4:29)

2. Keep away from profane and foolish discussions, which only drive people farther away from God. Such teaching is like an open sore that eats away the flesh. (2 Timothy 2:16–17)

3. My brothers, if someone is caught in any kind of wrongdoing, those of you who are spiritual should set him right; but you must do it in a gentle way. And keep an eye on yourselves, so that you will not be tempted, too. (Galatians 6:1)

Using Yesterday's News

When does news become history? By definition yesterday's newspaper is history. In reality most of us see history as what happened in the first half of our lives. The events in the last half of our lives are news—even if it is old news. Illustrations about events that have happened in the near past, or even more distant past if it was a well-known event, help tie the message of God's Word to the lives of people. Sometimes current news includes past events, especially on anniversaries involving the news of long ago. Let me suggest a few old news illustrations that will still be remembered by many people today and therefore help them apply the Scripture message to life.

1. During the Gulf War, Sadam Hussein announced he was beginning the mother of all battles. His term easily translated into American understanding. The following Easter my sermon was "The Mother of All Resurrections."

2. On the day the Oklahoma City Federal Building was bombed, most people assumed it had been done by foreign terrorists. We were shocked to hear that Timothy McVeigh was charged with the crime. Not only was he an American, but he was a white, middle-class, ex-military man who looked like the kid who grew up next door. We were shocked to realize he thought he was acting for us. He had heard people speak against our government in angry and violent terms. The people who used the words would not have used the bomb. But McVeigh took them at their word. He thought they would regard him as a hero. A similar thing happened in the racial struggles of the South. Members of the Klu Klux Klan burned buildings and killed people. They thought they had the support of groups such as the White Citizens Council and the John Birch Society who talked violence and urged the preservation of racial segregation. The White Citizens Council members were leading figures in many small communities—the bankers, politicians, clergy, and business people. They threw no bombs and killed no people, but they wrote the script for the KKK to do the violence. We need to say to ourselves: We know we are not terrorists, but are we carriers?

3. Babe Ruth hit 715 home runs in his baseball career. He also struck out 1,330 times. As we evaluate people, we often look for the truths that prove our point. We count the home runs of the people we like; and the strikeouts of those we don't like. Can we see others and ourselves

as we are—people with both home runs and strikeouts, people who are both sinners and saints?

4. In April 1961 Yuri Gagarin became the first human to travel in space. Khrushchev, the leader of the Soviet Union, announced to the world they had proven there is no God. "We have sent a man into space to look for God," Khrushchev said, "and we did not see him." Later a story spread across the Soviet Union, and then to the world. It was about a worm that met another worm deep down in the soil. The first worm said, "There is no Khrushchev." "How do you know?" asked the second worm. "Because," said the first, "I poked my head above the ground and I did not see him."

5. Elvis Presley may have much more influence on the United States and other parts of the world now than during his lifetime. A recent anniversary of his death attracted wide media attention and brought the singer back as current news. To many people, Presley has become a spiritual leader and is seen as a modern-day prophet, even though he made no attempt to be a religious leader and left no spiritual writings. Many can wonder how he can attract such a cultlike following. We can see this adoration of Elvis as a part of a desire for a spiritual life without a living God. In our world, many people identify themselves as spiritual and add, "But I don't mean religion." They want to develop their own spirituality that has no requirements, no duties, and no commitments. As Christians, we see our spirituality as a gift from God. The Holy Spirit gives us a new spirit through Jesus Christ. That Spirit calls us to repentance, gives us forgiveness, and sends us to serve.

6. Recently, the Public Broadcasting System did a series on several American presidents, including Harry Truman. Truman was a racist from his childhood. His family, his community, and his church promoted racial divisions. In his personal life and language he expressed racists

views. However, when he became the president of the United States, he knew he was president of all the people. He racially integrated the armed forces. He was the first president to introduce Civil Rights legislation to Congress. He changed the political map of the Deep South. He admitted that Harry Truman was a racist but that President Truman had a higher responsibility. As Christians we also can live above ourselves. The power of Christ lifts us above our own desires and abilities.

THE REST OF THE NEWS

The news comes under a big umbrella that includes lots of information and ideas which are not exactly news. Newspapers have many advice columnists on all subjects. The TV networks are introducing more and more "Magazines on the Air" programs. Many of these things can become sermon illustrations. Let me illustrate with several suggestions you may use for your own understanding of the news, as a part of a discussion group, and as a way to collect illustrations for a sermon.

1. Select one issue of your local paper (or the nearest large daily paper) and pretend the proverbial space alien uses that paper to learn about your community's concept of God. Look through the paper to see how God and other religious ideas are presented. Don't miss the obituary column, the horoscope, comics, church and other ads, and of course the news and editorials. Would the space alien learn about the God you worship?

2. Invite members of a Bible class or everyone in the congregation to clip news items that speak about religion other than on the religion page or in news submitted by church groups. Tell everyone to put the highlighted clippings on a bulletin board.

3. For an illustration that comes after a sermon: During the sermon, ask people to watch for news items about spe-

cific subjects. Again, suggest a place for the highlighted clippings to be posted. Possible subjects:

a. People killed or injured by handguns.

b. People killed or injured by misuse of drugs, including alcohol.

c. Ads that promote greed, anger, lust, etc.

d. People who do special acts of kindness for others—especially for strangers.

e. People who refer to their faith in stories about other subjects.

4. Use a page of the Sunday bulletin to write news articles about the lessons for the day—especially the texts. Write a headline and tell the news. Include an editorial.

THAT'S THE NEWS FOR TONIGHT

Information from the media is one of your best sources of sermon illustrations because a new set of stories comes out each day. As you hear or read them, others are doing the same. Look at each news item as an opportunity for you to put in the Jesus part.

CHAPTER 9

How to Use the Obvious Illustrations

All people who speak, even in private conversations, use illustrations. We want to explain our thoughts. We want others to understand us. We understand other people better when they use illustrations; so we do the same thing.

This chapter looks at those illustrations that we use by doing what comes naturally. The first purpose is to say, as they do in Australia, "Good on you, mate!" You have many natural skills as a communicator, and sometimes you need to take the time to be grateful for them.

However, like all natural skills, you can improve your use of the illustrations that just happen. You can become more aware of your natural abilities and make more use of them. You can fine-tune them to make better use of them.

You as an Illustration

One of your best sermon illustrations is you as a person. You believe in Jesus Christ. You know you are a sinner saved by grace. You don't have to point to yourself each time, but the way you speak of such subjects shows how they apply to your own life. One person (as a joke) said he quit preaching because the congregation insisted he had to refer to "we sinners" rather than "you sinners." I hope you don't have that problem. Notice how the prophets in the Old Testament and the apostles in the New frequently refer to their own experiences. They admit their own sins as they apply the Law to others. They confess their own faith as they preach the Gospel to others. They thank God for their own blessings as they lead others to an attitude of gratitude. Their message to us says God's Word works in their lives. As we pass the message on, we are telling others that the Word also works in our lives. By the way, the Scripture writers also reveal their weaknesses and struggles. They illustrate the fact that faith is always a struggle. We can do the same.

You are also a unique person. I say that not because I am a prophet or a psychic, but because each person is unique. Often we don't recognize that we are unique because we are so used to our own uniqueness, it seems normal to us. I had a hard time learning to say that I am a creative person. I realize it is a spiritual gift, and I use the gift that way. When I learned from 1 Corinthians 12:7 that my gift of creativity was of no value unless I used it for the good of all and that I need the special gifts that God has given others for my benefit, I came out of the closet as a creative person. I recognize the gift was there even in my early childhood. I hope you've already worked through the process that I struggled with. If not, this chapter is for you. If you have, this chapter is to encourage you to make even greater used of your special gifts in your sermons. I am going to list some of the obvious ones. Some of these gifts I have—many I do not. Long ago I learned someone in the congregation had the gifts that I lacked, so I let them use their gifts in my sermons. Perhaps you can do the same.

1. The gift of creativity: People are creative in different ways. I see my own creativeness in visual thinking and in seeing stories in the lives of people. I need to depend on others who have the same or different creative gifts. Using the creative work of others is also a gift. I have marveled at the ability that many have to use my children's sermons and make them more effective than I did. I depend on you to have the ability to use at least

some of my ideas in this book. Without your gift, mine would be of no use.

2. The gift of art: If you have a gift in graphic arts, you have a built-in resource for illustrations. You might do sketches for a sermon as you preach and develop a picture as you develop the sermon. You might also make your own illustrations as you prepare a sermon. I have limited artistic skills, but I solved that problem long ago—I married an artist. My wife has contributed a lot to my sermons by her artistic skills. If not a spouse, you can find artists in your congregation who will help make illustrations for you. The artistic illustrations and charts used in a sermon may be posted somewhere in the church area as a continued visual reminder of the sermon in which it was used.

3. The gift of music: A person with the ability to sing can use that gift in a sermon. Instead of quoting a hymn stanza as an illustration, sing it. The melody adds another memory contact to the idea just as a visual aid does. If you use a musical instrument, play it, and let the congregation join in singing. This is an obvious place where you can use the gift that others have when you lack it.

4. The gift of storytelling: Stories as sermon illustrations were discussed in a previous chapter. If you have the gift, consider telling the story of a text as an introduction to a sermon. If you don't have the gift, find a storyteller in your congregation who can tell the story as an introduction. Have someone tell a story from one of the lessons as a prelude to the worship service. Later, when the people hear the reading, it will have more meaning to them and they will remember it.

5. The gift of using puppets: Puppets are often used for children's sermons, but they work equally well for any sermon. The puppet offers an opportunity to present an opposing point of view. The puppet can get away with saying things you cannot.

6. The gift of magic: Some people have the gift of the sleight-of-hand tricks. These can be used effectively in a sermon, not as entertainment, but as ways to show conflict and mystery.

7. The gift of special experiences: Maybe you've had another career, grew up under special circumstances, had a special problem or blessing, or other experiences. Such things may give you a special insight to a text or a special understanding of a needed application. The first time I heard a blind pastor preach I was delighted that he used a visual aid. His lack of sight made the visual aid more effective for me. Tell the congregation why you see the text as you do. Encourage them to use their special experiences to help understand a text.

8. The gift of humor: Like other gifts this one cannot be faked. If you have it, use it.

9. The gift of gifts: This list has no end. The point is for you to evaluate yourself and listen to the evaluation of others. If you have an ace in communication, play it!

One other thing about you that may give you a lot of illustrations for your sermons: You make mistakes. You already know that, but do you realize a lot of church members think you've got everything under control? Instead of hiding your mistakes, or worse yet, pretending you never make any, acknowledge anything that goes wrong and put the mistake under the Gospel.

My brother told me a wonderful story. He was the godfather for a Baptism in a congregation that had a new pastor just out of the seminary. He remembered that the sermon was okay, but he was glad to be a part of the Baptism and maybe didn't pay as much attention as he should have. As the service was about to end, right before the Benediction, the pastor announced that he had forgotten a part of his sermon. He said it was an important part of the message and he wanted them to hear it. And they did! My brother remembered that part. The idea worked so well for him that I considered using it as a tactic, but that didn't seem fair to me. I make enough mistakes on my own; so I don't need to fake any.

THE CONGREGATION AS AN ILLUSTRATION

Just as you are an illustration to your congregation, the members of the church are an illustration to you and to each other. As you study your text, you also study your people. When Jesus was talking about sowing seeds and catching fish, his hearers did not think he was using an illustration. He was talking about what they talked about. It worked for them.

Let's look at a number of characteristics of your congregation to help you use them as natural illustrations in your sermons.

1. The first one is easy—just to help you get the idea. When you are speaking to your congregation, how do you refer to the place where they live? Do you say house, apartment, mobile home, condo, or apartment? In some congregations all, or almost all, of the people would live in one of the abodes listed. In others, the answer is all of the above. In that case, you refer to their homes. Illustrations that use experiences about homes reach people where they spend most of their time. Try this one on yourself: Think of the place where you lived when you were a small child. You probably saw yourself in the kitchen, bedroom, or other family section of the house. Now think of a home where you were an occasional guest as a child. You probably saw yourself at the dining room table or in the living room, the part of the house for guests. Now think of the church you attended as a child. Do you remember only being in the worship service? Or, do you also remember the classrooms, churchyard, social hall, or basement? Ask those who worship: Will you remember this church only as a place of worship, where you were like a guest? Or, will you remem-

ber it as a place where you lived and where you share experiences with others in the church family?

2. Now look at the occupations of people in your congregation. In some parishes, a majority of the people share the same type of work. If you use only illustrations about that kind of work, the others may feel left out. However, the minority is always used to hearing the majority's agenda. You also need to remember the pre- and post career people, those who are students, and those who are retired. Look for illustrations that help people bridge gaps and understand the needs of others. One did not have to be a fisherman to understand Jesus' stories about fishing. However, it helped if you knew others who did fish for a living.

3. What does *family* mean to the people who hear your sermons? Are those with father, mother, and children a minority? What percentage of the adults are single? (In the congregation from which I recently retired, 40 percent of the people on the church council were single.) How many single-parent families are in your congregation? How many people are raising their grandchildren? When you refer to families, use illustrations from the variety of families included in your parish.

4. I'm going to give an extreme picture of a congregation. All of the members grew up in that congregation, as did their parents before them. Most are related to one another. They are alike in their financial, educational, and vocational status. It is easy to speak to such a group as a group because one illustration fits all. However, you may want to use illustrations to deal with three specific issues:

   a. Such a congregation needs to be reminded that their unity comes from Jesus Christ, not from blood relationships and a community nest.

   b. Members of such a congregation need to be aware of the Holy Christian Church. They need to know they are one in Christ with people of other races, nationalities, and social status. Other Christians need the security that such a congregation has to give. They need the diversity that other Christians can give.

c. The youth in such a congregation need to be aware of a broader world. If and when they leave that community, they must be prepared for many changes—including in the church. I have found that people who have always been a member of the same congregation with the same pastor for years, have a difficult time when they move to a new community and new church. We can help people be ready for the move by our illustrations from the world beyond the local parish.

5. Now for the opposite extreme: Do you serve a congregation where few, if any, of the people are related by blood to others? Are most of your members new to the congregation, and do they know they will be there for a limited time? Do the members of the congregation seldom see each other outside of church activities? Illustrations can also help members of such a church be aware of important issues.

a. They need to create a local family for holidays, birthdays, and other social activities. The congregation offers that family as a part of the unity in Christ that they share. They cannot take their local family for granted, but must be open to receive the hospitality of others and to offer their hospitality to others.

b. They are needed in the congregation during the time they live in the community. Even though they are new, they are not guests, and they need not go through an initiation period before they can serve in all congregational functions.

c. By being involved in the congregation where they now live, they will be better equipped to get involved in another congregation when they move on to the next job.

When they move away, they will know they did something worthwhile in this church.

6. What is special about your community? Where I grew up, a sermon about Paul's thorn in the flesh would have brought to mind a blackberry briar or a locust tree. Where I live now, a cactus would be a better illustration. You can eat at a fast-food place anywhere in the country and get the exact same food. Churches are not fast-food places. They are homes, and home cooking adjusts to the local customs. Illustrations are a good way to adapt your universal message to a neighborhood congregation.

In all the situations above, and in the others you will think of, see two ways to use sermon illustrations. One is comfortable for the congregation. They understand it because it comes from their experience. It is homemade. The other way is to use illustrations to challenge the congregation to see beyond themselves. It helps them see and understand the needs and experiences of others. It is an import from another culture.

THE BUILDING AS AN ILLUSTRATION

One of the most obvious sources of illustrations, but one that is (from my experience) frequently ignored, is the house of worship itself. No matter whether you preach in a traditional Gothic church, a modern architectural monument, or a rented storefront, the building offers many illustrations. The great advantage of using illustrations from your house of worship is that you give meanings to the building itself and the congregation builds a repertoire of illustrations that become a part of their every week worship experience. When I served a congregation with a modest but attractive building, our youth group went caroling early on Christmas Eve. Instead of singing for our own members and receiving cookies from them, we sang in a nearby very low-income area. After we sang at each home, we gave gifts to the family from members of our congregation. People from the poor community gathered and invited us to join them in their church for singing. Their house of worship had been a store. It needed repairs. Later, when we were back at our own house of worship for a Christmas Eve service, all of us realized that the other place of worship was more like the place where Jesus was born. Having worshiped in the storefront building became a great Christmas worship experience for us.

I'm going to list a number of good illustrations that are often a part of a church building. All of them will not be in your church, but you will have others not on my list.

1. The New Testament church did not have a house of worship. Many still worshiped in parts of the Jewish temple; most worshiped in homes or outside. Peter talks about a building, but it is made of living stones. (See 1 Peter 2:4–5.) Believers are united to be a spiritual temple. If your building is made of brick or stone (perhaps you could even refer to boards and other building materials), ask each person to pick out one brick. That brick is you. The mortar holding us together is Jesus Christ. We are a spiritual temple because he has brought us together. When you come to church, look at your brick and then glance at the other bricks. Now look at the other people who worship with you. Each time we are together, we are reminded we are one in Christ. During a building project one congregation invited all members to write their names on the backsides of the stack of bricks that were to become a part of a wall. The people had a permanent illustration that they experienced each time they worshiped there.

2. Many churches have altars as a reminder of the altar in the Old Testament place of worship. The Israelites used the altar as a place to sacrifice animals, the sacrifice demanded by God as the price of sin (to be followed by God's forgiveness). Christians have a cross on, above, or nearby their altars to say the sacrifice to pay for sin has

been made by Christ. Instead of coming to the altar to bring a sacrifice (a holy gift to God), we come to the altar to receive the Sacrament (a holy gift from God).

3. We use two different kinds of altars. Many of them look like tables. They remind us that Jesus and his disciples gathered for a meal on the night the Lord gave them his supper. Other altars look like the tombs in which people were once buried. When Christians were persecuted in Rome, they worshiped in the catacombs, the underground burial places. As a matter of convenience they used the tombs as a place to put the bread and wine as they prepared to receive the body and blood of Christ. This became an illustration of how Christ faced death as he was buried and defeated death by his resurrection. When the Christians moved topside, they brought the illustration with them as they made altars to look like tombs.

4. Many churches have stained-glass windows. The earliest use of stained glass in churches was not only for architectural beauty, but also as visual aids. At a time when few people were literate and the worship service, including the sermon, was in a language the people did not understand, the stories of the Bible were told in stained-glass windows. These were picture sermons. In modern times many do not appreciate the overly ornate cathedrals of the past. However, all of the windows and carvings were teaching aids then as videos, picture books, and posters are today. Then, and now, someone had to explain the messages of the stained-glass windows. If your church has such windows—even many modern houses of worship do—use the windows as illustrations in the story. If a window tells a story from the Bible, identify the story in glass with the story in the Bible. If your windows have symbols, explain the symbols when they apply to a sermon's message. Once the message of the window is explained, you can refer to it in future sermons and continue to build an understanding of the work of art.

5. Your church may just have windows—as in those that let the light in and let us look out. They also can be illustrations. I recognize this is unusual, but the entire chancel wall of my last church was glass. Those who worshiped looked out on the Catalina Mountains. We used Psalm 121 often, especially for confirmation services, as a way to see that our help came from the Lord who made the mountain. We also saw other things out of the window that may be more ordinary. Airplanes and hot air balloons flew by. Birds landed on the sills. We could see a few homes and another church building. All of these things helped get the message outside of our church into the daily lives of people. Even if those inside cannot see out of a window, point them toward it and remind them of the world out there that needs the message from in here.

6. Many congregations with communion rails in the chancel also have a gate or some device to add more space when the Lord's Supper is served. When I first saw ushers close one of those gates, I didn't like the symbolism. It appeared to me that they had closed the chancel that had been opened when the curtain split at the death of Christ. But Psalm 24 changed the symbolism for me—and became a sermon. The psalm asks who can go up the Holy Hill? Who will enter God's holy temple? Close the gate and consider the possible answers. The psalm also gives the answer. Those who are pure in what they say and do will go through the gate. I guess we don't get through—but wait! The psalm also tells us the Lord will bless us and will declare us innocent. He will open the gate for us. "Fling wide the gates, open the ancient doors, and the great king will come in. Who is the great king? He is the Lord, strong and mighty, the Lord victorious in battle" (Psalm 24:7–8).

7. Banners have become the stained glass windows in our time. Banners have a lot of advantages. They can be

changed according to the seasons and other special events. You can put a banner in the chancel when it is first used and let it be an illustration that stays in the place of worship to keep a message before the people. Those who worship may make banners and know they are taking an active part in worship. Sunday school and vacation Bible school classes can make banners and bring their families to church to see them. Banners can be made of paper and used only once, or can be works of art that take hours of labor and expensive material. The latter kind can hang around for a while. In all cases, put meaning into the words, pictures, and symbols on the banners. Encourage families to make a similar banner for their own homes.

8. The cross is the focal point of Christian worship and most church buildings include a cross. Help your congregation see the meaning of each cross. The crucifix reminds us of Christ's suffering and death. The empty cross shows his victory over death. A processional cross may be used to lead people to and from worship. Explain any other special purpose of a cross used in the building.

9. Offering plates are everyday tools in worship services, but they may also be illustrations. Remind the people that they all bring offerings from their source of income. The offerings come from salaries, allowances, investments, retirement funds, and savings. They come from people who can give a lot in terms of dollars and those who can give only a little. But all of the offerings come together into one gift to God. Put the plates on the altar to show how we offer our individual gifts as one gift to God. We all share in the work of ministry.

10. Candles are used in most places of worship. Candles can be an illustration of Jesus as the Light of the world. Candles can be reminders of the gifts of the Holy Spirit. Sometimes a special candle is used for a Baptism. Some

candles are used only when the Lord's Supper is a part of the worship. Advent candles are an illustration for the special season of the church year. Sometimes congregations get in the habit of using such things, and they become a habit that has no meaning. Candles should be a natural illustration to illuminate a point of a sermon. Does it help you to watch the candles be lighted at the beginning of the service and to remember that God's Word is a light to our path? (See Psalm 119:105.) Later when you hear the word, could the candles remind you to use that Word to guide your life? When the candles are extinguished at the end of the service, would it help you to think that the light is not being put out, but rather it is being transferred to your life as you go back to your family and work?

11. Look at the floor plan of your place of worship. Does it have a message to illustrate Christian doctrine? Are you gathered around the altar as people of God gathered at a meal? Can you see the cross as you look up at the ceiling and realize the altar is at the place where the arms of the cross meet? This is a special story about the church I served before I retired. Maybe you can adapt it to your building or find another similar illustration. Four large and visible beams come together at the center of the ceiling. The beams are held together by a massive metal frame that could have been used as an altar. The architect explained to me, and I to the congregation, that the building was overengineered. The beams and the metal frame did not have to be that big. They were made that way to give a feeling of strength—the strength we have in Jesus Christ. When we moved into the house of worship, I told the story and added, "All of you have a brother-in-law or a neighbor who says he can't come to church because the roof would fall in. Invite them and tell them we are prepared—neither the roof nor the message will be damaged by their presence." That was 16 years ago and occasional-

ly someone will tell me, "You're right! My brother-in-law came on Easter and the roof didn't fall in."

12. Many church buildings have a side seating area, a choir section, or other place you can designate as a jury box for a special illustration. Stand before that jury box as you present the part of the sermon about the court of justice. Present the evidence. Look for defenses against our guilt and causes for mitigation. Then move from the court of justice to the throne of grace. Go before the altar and plead for mercy through Jesus Christ. Forget the defenses. Don't blame others. Instead, depend on Jesus Christ to defend you and all others.

13. If you wear vestments during a church service, they also can be used to illustrate the work you do and other special meanings. One time I met a woman with four children through counseling. I had visited the family several times in their home and knew the children well. When they came to church the first time, one child asked (in a very loud voice), "Why are you wearing a dress?" Since then I have found reasons to explain my "uniform" and to use the colors and symbols as illustrations.

14. Flowers are often used in worship services. Some may think of them as decorations, why don't you think of them as illustrations? The poinsettias at Christmas and lilies at Easter have obvious symbolic meanings. Other flowers can also add to the message of a sermon. Many people provide flowers for a church service for special meanings: celebration of a birthday or anniversary, in memory of a loved one, or thanksgiving of a special event. Perhaps those experiences are a part of a sermon on the same Sunday. Connect the sight and smell of the flowers to the message and you have a good illustration. Some churches have live plants in the chancel. I used a plant for a sermon from John 15:5, "I am the vine, and you are the branches." Perhaps I overdid it by pruning the ficus fig (verse 2) because one member told me that

it was not the right time of the year. However, the ficus fig survived and with a toy snake in its branches worked well for a sermon on Genesis 3 about the first temptation. If there are no plants in your place of worship, you can borrow them from members. A Christmas tree and its decorations provide many illustrations for sermons during the Advent/Christmas/Epiphany season.

15. Many congregations have chrismons for the Christmas tree. Many chrismons are symbols of Old Testament stories, events from the life of Jesus, and events from the life of the church. They may be used all year by matching the chrismon with the church year or with the Scripture readings used in the worship service. Find a place in the church where chrismons may be displayed all year, and change them according to the season.

16. Spend some time sitting in the back of your church to look at it from the point of view of those who hear your sermons. What other illustrations do you see? Do you have flags that could be used as illustrations on a national holiday? What could you illustrate with the baptismal font? I visited a church recently that has a baptismal font with a pump so those who worship can hear the flow of water. That would be an excellent illustration, not only for Baptism, but also for Psalm 23 as we lead people to the still waters. Would the light fixtures in your church make good illustrations as well as good illumination? Look at the organ pipes, musical instruments, and other things that people see regularly. They are all available for the using.

17. The most throwaway item in your church is the Sunday bulletin. However, it is first a take-home item. Members often take the bulletin home because it gives the schedule of events for the week. You can add another reason to take it home if it is an illustration in your sermon. Many congregations use a bulletin service that provides a picture illustrating one of the readings for the day.

Sometimes the bulletin cover includes a quote from a Bible reading. These are natural illustrations often missed by those who only look inside for the news. You can give them reasons to keep the picture on the refrigerator door or other visible spot at home. You can also make your own bulletin cover—at least on special occasions—as a part of your sermon. An artist in the congregation can provide a picture. Computers provide many ways to make charts, pictures, and designs that could be used to illustrate ideas in the sermon, also allowing the people to take home with them.

18. I have suggested many ways to use the furniture and décor of many churches as illustrations. Now let's look at the things in your church that might be called secular—the kind of things that are in most buildings. The lighted exit signs required by law in most places can illustrate a lot of things about life. Some churches have emergency lighting,—you can work with that. Locks on doors, light switches, and thermostats go unnoticed to most people. But if they are used to illustrate something, they add to the spiritual message of the building. If you worship in a place that was not built as a church, do not feel sorry for yourself. Instead, use what is available to illustrate how God's Word applies to all of life. I have preached in a theater, a Quonset hut, a fire hall, a funeral home, a community center, and a store basement. Some of these were not the best places to lead worship, but each gave a sense of reality to the Word we used there.

I've had fun making the above list because it brought back many wonderful memories of being with people in worship. The list turned out longer than I expected. I also realize I missed many opportunities to use good illustrations because they were so obvious that I didn't notice them. I hope you can pick up where I left off.

THE EXTRA SOUND TRACK

Sounds are an important part of a worship service. Think of the voices that preach, lead the worship, read the lessons, and pray. Hear the music of voices and instruments. I always thought stereo meant having two speakers, so a worship service was in stereo when it used music and the spoken word. But stereo is three-dimensional. Think of a third sound track in the worship service. That track carries all the other special sounds that add to a worship service.

1. Listen to the sounds you don't want. Is there an American Airline's jet headed for Chicago that flies over your church every Sunday just as you start the sermon? Is your church near a busy road with heavy traffic—even on Sunday morning? Such sounds are annoying and can distract both the preacher and those who listen. This is an opportunity to turn a lemon into lemonade. Stop the sermon when the sound interferes. Use the extraneous sound as an illustration. The world will always try to drown out the Word of God. If we use earplugs to block out the other sounds, we also block out God's Word. If you stop and say your message is important for those who are there, the distraction will have become an advantage.

2. The sound of a siren always means someone needs help. A building is on fire, someone has been injured, or someone has violated a law. Use the siren as a call to prayer. We pray for whoever needs help and for those who are providing the help.

3. This one may not happen often but it worked once for me. Our sound system was giving problems and picked up a police call during the sermon. I added, "You have now heard from the law. Let me speak for the Gospel." The honest truth is I don't remember the rest of that sermon.

4. I visited a church recently that had cascading water in the baptismal fountain. The fountain was either miked

or the church had such good acoustics that the sound of the moving water was in the background through the worship service. It was a constant reminder of our Baptism into Jesus Christ.

5. The musical instruments used to lead worship can also contribute to a sermon.

   a. Many psalm texts can use the blast of a trumpet or the clash of a cymbal.

   b. Check the organ for special sound effects. Many new organs have sounds you wouldn't use with music, but you might use as an illustration.

   c. Organ or piano music could be used to illustrate peace and conflict. You might have a difficult time to get some musicians to play the sour notes. Remind them music always gets the Gospel part; so this is a chance to do the Law.

   d. Think of many other sounds that add a memorable moment to a sermon: an alarm clock, a crying baby, a telephone ringing, a slammed door, the sound of traffic, a dog's bark. You can add to the list. All of these sounds can be taped and used during a sermon.

WATCH AND LISTEN FOR THE OBVIOUS

Illustrations are for the ears as well as the eyes. Learn to watch and to listen for the obvious. Then when you speak about the obvious, others will hear your words as something that fits into their lives. The phone system of my childhood was a collection of small, community companies, each with 12 to 18 families sharing the same line. All lines were connected in the nearby town at a place we called "Central." The lady that ran central knew all the people on all the lines because she had to listen. It was her job. Sometimes I think a parish pastor is like the person who was central. It's our job to listen. That means we need to know what not to tell, but a lot of what we hear needs to be told. Listen to the things on people's minds and in their conversations. Some things include weather, sports, politics, and most of all other people. People are more interested in hearing what other people in the community are saying than they are in the quotes of scholars, poets, and famous people in history.

When your eyes and ears are open to hear and see, you will have something to tell and show others.

CHAPTER 10

How to Listen to a Sermon

You've taken classes on how to prepare and preach a sermon. Few, if any, of the people in your congregation have been taught how to listen to a sermon. You are reading this book (which probably indicates you also use other homiletical resources), but those in the pew do not read books on listening to sermons, and only a small percentage have read a book of sermons.

Since you hope to preach a lot of sermons to the people in your congregation, and since they will hear a lot of sermons from you or someone else, wouldn't it be a good idea to teach people how to listen to a sermon? It could be a sermon in itself. A number of times I have done a variety of worship narrative services in which I explained the acts of worship as we did them. They were always well received by the congregation and reruns were requested. But until now, I never thought of doing the same on a sermon.

Perhaps this is a good opportunity to set an example for you and teach you how to read a book, at least this book. I'm not writing it because I think I am an expert on preaching. I am writing it because I have had a lot of experience on preaching in a great variety of situations. I don't have to know all the answers to help you work on your sermons. In fact, I may help you more by asking you the right questions. Your job is to pick the experiences from my ministry and the questions I ask that might help you in yours. Other things I have written will make you think about ways that will be better for you than the ways I have suggested. Finally, you can broaden your own understanding of preaching by recognizing that some things I suggested seem … well, dumb, to you. But I assure you that someone else may appreciate the idea you rejected.

The people who hear your sermons will have the same possible reactions to your sermons as you have to my book. Your faith, training, and experience will reach them, and they will benefit from your sermons because they reached them in their current situation. Others will feel you missed them once in a while, but you gave them God's Word, and they can make their own applications. There will be a few, once in a while, who occasionally think you had a bad sermon or—even worse—won't remember a word you said. Don't worry about it. Do the best you can and depend on the Holy Spirit to bless your work in the hearts of others. If it is of any comfort to you, Eutychus fell asleep while listening to a sermon preached by the apostle Paul. (See Acts 20:9.) Perhaps someone should fund a lecture series on homiletics and name it in honor of Eutychus.

Maybe we can help those who hear our sermons by teaching them how to listen to sermons. I have done it often by explaining certain parts of a sermon and assigning those who hear the sermon parts they are responsible for. I will make those kinds of suggestions. You can decide if you want to put it all together into one sermon.

WHAT DO YOU EXPECT FROM THOSE WHO HEAR YOU?

At a minimum, you probably want people to agree with you. That sounds good, but over the years I have found those who disagree with something I said in a sermon probably got more out of it than those who nod at everything I say. I don't think people should be trained to either cheer or boo a sermon, yet that often happens. They do not come to church as an audience, they are worshipers and learners.

Sometimes people will accept anything said from the pulpit without question, though that day is passing and I thank God. Often they agree because they don't understand or weren't paying attention. This happened in one of the churches I visited while working on this book. The pastor announced twe did not have to be members of the congregation to receive the Lord's Supper. The only requirements were that we love God with all our hearts and love our neighbors as ourselves. One of the reasons I want to receive communion often is I can't fully do either of the above. I thought they would have a cheap bread and wine bill that month because no one would go to the altar. But most of the people did receive communion. I don't think they understood what the pastor had said. Perhaps the pastor didn't either.

Next, we expect people to act on the Word they have heard. That sounds good too, and it is one of my expectations. But again, if all of us could do what the Word tells us to do, our sermons could be very short. My own expectations have grown over the years. Each one was a new step for me, so I'll share them with you in that order.

> I started thinking it was my job to preach *to* people, and I still think that. I am called by the congregation to preach God's Word to them so they may hear and learn what God says. That's a big assignment. I prepare a sermon with that goal in mind. I expect them to listen. I have learned I can help them listen. It's not enough I say the right things, I also want to know they hear the right things. When I preach to them, I am the teacher and they are the students. That is good, but it dawned on me that students are learning to do something. Was I making my church members into the spiritual equivalent of professional students?

> Next I learned to preach *for* people in the church. I had to speak for husbands to wives and for wives to husbands.

I had to speak for parents to children and for children to parents.

The Word does not belong only to me. God spoke to all of us. My position, training, and experience make me responsible to preach the Word. It is easy to preach to people in any congregation, but it is much easier to speak for people if you are their pastor because you know them and they know you. We speak for people when we offer correction, instruction, forgiveness, acceptance, and love. People need to be taught to hear the message not just from the pastors but from others as they speak for them. When the pastor speaks for the hungry, the pastor is not asking for food—those who are hungry are making the request. When the pastor speaks for the doubter or the unbeliever, the pastor is not asking for help—they are. People need to know how to listen to the message. They also need to know they have a voice in a sermon and the pastor can speak for them. We need to tell them. A man once asked me to speak his concerns about an issue to the congregation. I told him he had a good point and presented a good case. He told me that he knew he could become emotional and sound angry even if he was not. I was glad to speak for him. We need to let people know we are there to speak for them.

My next step was to speak *through* people. I realized I was not the only one in the congregation who had the ability and the responsibility to share the Gospel of Christ with others. My job was to equip the other saints to join in the sowing the seed of the Word. Therefore, I learned to prepare sermons for partners in ministry rather than for consumers. I am using the same concept as I work on this book. As I preached to people, I gave them a message they could pass on to others. When people tell me about sermons they have heard from others pastors, they most often start by telling me an illustration the other pastor used. Most often it is an object lesson or a story. But they tell you more than the illustration. In most cases they will remember why the illustration was used. The other pastor is preaching through them.

You need to let people know what you expect of them as you deliver a sermon. The more you can enlist them as partners in the ministry, the more they will get from your sermons for themselves.

WHAT DO THEY ALREADY KNOW ABOUT SERMONS?

Don't assume that your people all need Sermon Listening 101. Some of them have been listening to sermons longer than you have been preaching sermons. I believe I learned more about preaching from those who knew how to listen to sermons than I did from those who taught my homiletics classes. That is not a put-down to my seminary professors. They gave me the tools, but the people in my congregation showed me how to use those tools.

I heard a speaker address a group of 200 church-going people on Christian worship. He spoke as an expert telling them how to worship as though they were all new in the church. I knew many of those people and admired the depth of their worship. They may have learned something from the speaker, but he learned nothing from them. I think they had a lot to teach him. As you plan to teach your people how to listen to a sermon, start by finding those who already know, and listen to what they can teach you.

Early in my ministry, a semi-professional actress attended my church for one year. I missed her when she moved away because she was my communication checkpoint. When she heard the text, her face looked puzzled. When I explained something, she would sometimes nod approval—but not always. At other times, she would look confused. She never realized how she made my sermon into a dialog. I didn't tell her because I thought it might make her self-conscious. Most people are not that expressive, but the face often shows what is going on inside the head and heart.

One way to encourage people to use the ability they already have to listen to a sermon is to ask them to use their memories of previous sermons. Well-known texts are often repeated. Maybe people will remember what another pastor said about the text you are using. Christmas and Easter sermons start with the same message each year, but each year they gain a value-added quotient. Your sermon can reenforce previous sermons if you ask the people to use what they already know. I remember a sermon I preached on the text of the Prodigal Son when I had three teenage sons at home. Nine years later I used the text again and referred to the change in my views. People caught the message. Those who had children leave home understood the change. Those with young children were prepared for the experience.

Elsewhere in this book is a sermon "When the Irresistible Force Meets the Immovable Object," based on the miracle at Nain. Following the sermon, a woman painted a picture to show a grave as described in the sermon. Her artwork may not have made a juried show, but she got an *A* in sermon listening.

HOW TO LISTEN TO A TEXT

Your goals in a sermon:
1. Apply a text to the lives of the people who hear it. Or,

2. Help the people who hear the text apply it to themselves.

I switched from 1 to 2 early in my ministry. There are some obvious reasons—and some less obvious.

> No preacher can apply the text to each person who attends church. Our people have a great variety of problems and guilt. They have a variety of abilities and opportunities. They need to hear the Word so they can apply it to their own lives. We who preach can make generic applications, but those who listen must put on the brand names. If the preacher makes all the applica-

tions, those who hear the sermon may say, "That doesn't apply to me." However, if the preacher leaves some of the application open-ended, the hearers can say, "How does that apply to me?"

I didn't know the needs of all the people who hear my sermons. I loved making housecalls, and many people came to my office for pastoral care. From those contacts I could understand a lot, but not everything, about those people. I also realized for every person who shared a person situation with me, X number of others had the same situation but were not able, or felt no need, to share it. I had to offer a word of the Law that reached beyond the sins I knew about. I had to offer the forgiveness of sins far beyond those confessed to me. I had to offer the challenge of Christian service far beyond what people offered to do on the stewardship committee's talent survey. I had to depend on the Word to do the work.

Finally, I realized many people who attended church got the Word only through me. This scares me, but check it out. Many good, active church members receive the majority, if not all, of their Word intake for the week from their pastors. In many cases, pastors and parishioners have created a codependence. The church members depend on the pastors to provide the Word for them, and the pastors depend on the church member to depend on them.

One way to help people learn how to listen to a sermon is to help them learn how to use God's Word. They know the pastor will use a text for the sermon. You can help them by publishing the sermon text and other biblical readings for next week in this week's bulletin. Only a small percentage will use that information. Some will use those readings for family devotions. Others will read the lessons privately. You can encourage people to prepare for next week's worship by including a promo either in your sermon, the announcements, or in the bulletin. No one method will reach all people. Use the idea of listing the readings in the bulletin as one way to get people to study the Bible. It's easier to have a variety of ways of involving people with different interests than to find one way that fits the needs of everyone.

Next, help people see the connection between your sermon and the text. I've heard (and preached) sermons that were textual, but those who heard it thought it came from the pastor rather than the Scriptures. The pastor did all the chewing on the Word, and the people were expected to do the swallowing. This doesn't mean that you need to give chapter and verse for each use of the Scripture; though you should be prepared to do so for those wonderful people who ask. Here are some ways to hand the text to the people as you preach.

> Encourage people to bring their Bibles to church. I was not successful at this, but I still think it is the best. When they have their own Bible in hand as you preach, they can mark sections for future use. They also have their choice of a translation that speaks the way they do. By finding each text and other biblical references they learn their way through the Bible without needing to look at the table of contents.

> Next best, have Bibles in the pews. The advantage is that all will be using the same translation and you can give page numbers to help people find the text. Sometimes you can ask people to read a section with you. Of course, that requires that everyone have the same translation.

> Use a bulletin service that provides the reading of the day or copy the text into the bulletin so those who listen can also read. Again, they can mark parts of the text that they want to remember. They also can take it home with them. The disadvantage is they don't get the experience of learning how to find their way through Route 66—a pun on the number of books in the Bible.

> Pick a key verse or thought from the text you will emphasize in your sermon. Have an artist or a computer expert make it into a small poster. You can use this on the cover of your bulletin or as an insert. From my point of view,

this is a modern-day method of memory work. The visual of the words will help people remember them. The message does not have to be an exact quote from the text. For a sermon on 1 Corinthians 13 I had a bulletin insert that said, "If you can't do it with love, don't do it." After that I frequently saw the message in the homes of members. It was on refrigerator doors, bulletin boards, above the kitchen sink, and (at least in one case) in a bedroom.

Many times translations will offer a variety of ways to give the meaning of a key section of a text. Rather than pick one as right and prove the others are wrong, put a list of the various translations in the bulletin. The collection of translations gives a three-dimensional view of the text and helps people understand that no one translation can include the variety of possible meanings.

The items listed above are methods. The goal is to help people use God's Word in their lives. Look for ways to teach people to use the Word for themselves. Bible classes are great, and may their numbers increase. However, in most congregations you will reach many more people through sermons than through Bible classes.

After I had been in a congregation for a year, I asked the elders for an evaluation of my ministry. A number of them gave positive and encouraging remarks, then one said, "I don't see you as much of a preacher." I thought to myself, "And I asked for this!" Fortunately, I listened to the rest of his comment. He came from a church background that made him think of preaching as legalistic and authoritarian. He said he heard my sermons as helping him rather than condemning him. I was teaching him to be responsible. That elder is one of many laypeople who contributed to my ministry—and to this book.

We help people use the Word when we preach sermons that make people accountable to God, not to us. If they find comfort and help, it comes from God's Word, not us. Or, if they have something to fuss about, their argument is with the Word, not the preacher.

A Word of Explanation

Fifteen years ago a friend gave me *Foxfire 7*. (Edited with an introduction by Paul F. Gillespie. Anchor PressDoubleday, Garden City, New York, 1982.) This book is a part of the Foxfire series that was a study of the culture of the Appalachian area of the United States. Other volumes were about farming, building log cabins, butchering, etc. Volume 7 was a study of the religion in the area. The sociology students who conducted the study avoided denominational leaders, and in most cases clergy. From a business point of view, they were looking for the consumers' point of view about religion, rather than the production perspective. They went to homes, barber shops, town squares, and other gathering places of people and asked what they got out of their religion. Sad for me, my denomination is not well represented in that area. However, I could see a difference in what members of other denominations believed and did and what their denomination taught and expected. I know that difference would also be a part of the members of my denomination. The following three points in this chapter are based on my understanding and application of *Foxfire 7*.

How to Hear the Law

Much of my seminary training was spent on how to use, and not to use, the Law. I like the King James Version translation of 1 Timothy 1:8, "But we know that the law is good, if a man use it lawfully." For this section I want to paraphrase that to read, "But we know that the law is good, if a man hear it lawfully."

Teach your people to know how to listen to the Law with an illustration from the numerous biblical references to our two natures. By our human nature we are enemies of God and spiritually dead. The illustration is that our human nature has control of one ear. All that we hear through that ear is received as coming from the Enemy. Of course, the fact that we are spiritually dead means the human nature ear is often deaf and won't even get the message of God's Law.

But we have another ear. Because the Holy Spirit has given us a new life through faith in Jesus Christ, we are God's friends. The ear of our new nature hears God's Law as a Christian. Jesus' marching orders to his followers told them repentance must be preached in his name to all people. (See Luke 24:47.) A message of the Law goes through the ear of the old nature. However, the same message of the Law in Christ's name goes through the ear of the new nature.

You as a preacher need to know that the people in the pew are going to hear your Law messages with both ears. Tell them about the two ears so they can be aware of their spiritual hearing problems. When any of us listen to the Law through our human nature ear, we will have one or more of the following reactions:

> That doesn't apply to me. He's talking to those other people.

> I can't be blamed for that because I was born this way. I didn't choose to _____.

> It's not my fault. My parents, church leaders, God, or someone else made me do it.

> I did more good than bad; so what's the problem?

> The sermon is right! I'm so bad, God couldn't love me.
> My sins are worse than anyone else's.

Notice these are human responses and do not involve faith. People who do not know Christ have no other choice than to deal with sins on their own. That means they have to ignore, defend, excuse, or deny sin. Even those of us who believe still have the human nature ear. We can have those responses—even when the spoken message includes Christ. The fear ear can tune out the faith ear. When we hear a message of God's Law through our sinful nature's ear, it drives us away from Christ.

Now let's see how the ear of our new Christian nature hears a Law message. Even if the speaker does not mention the Gospel of Christ, the believer hears the message of the Law coming in the name of Christ. Jesus came to obey the Law in our place. By his death, he took away the guilt of the Law. Therefore, we do not need to deny, defend, or excuse our sins. He has taken them away. The ear of our new nature still hears the Law and responds. The response:

Repentance.

That's a short list. The beauty of faith is that we don't negotiate conditions of our forgiveness. We can't promise we will stop sinning. We can't tell God we'll pay him back by doing good. We do not have, and do not need, a way to build up good points with God to pay off the demerits. The good we do is a part of our relationship with God. There is no way to earn bonus points. (See Luke 17:7–10.) When we hear God's Law through our new nature's ear, we return to Christ in repentance.

How to Hear the Gospel

Those of us who believe in Christ want to hear the Gospel over and over again. We need to hear that Christ still loves us and is with us. We need to hear his voice as he leads us here on earth. However, when we come to hear God's Word with our good ear, the ear of our human nature comes along.

Our sinful nature can hear the words of the Gospel but not with the ears of faith. Be aware of some of the ways those who do not believe in Christ hear the message about him. Also, know that even we Christians can listen with the wrong ear and get the wrong message. Without faith, they listen to the Gospel and say one or more of the following:

> Just like I've always said. It makes no difference what you believe as long as you are sincere.

> If Jesus paid for all my sins, that means I can sin all I want and he will still forgive me.

If God loves everyone, then it's no big deal to have him on your side. I don't think some people deserve God's love.

I know Jesus died for me so I don't need the Bible, the church, and all those people who do nothing but go to church.

I don't believe that stuff about Jesus, but I like the people, the music, and I think the church is good for the kids.

Weak people need a God who died for them. I'll take care of myself.

I was baptized (born again) 30 years ago. That's good enough for me.

The ear of our new nature in Christ receives a different message. It hears that God sent his Son to be human to die for us. It hears that Christ rose again and is with us as we live and die; so we also will be raised from the dead. The response:

I believe.

Again the list is very short. I know you could add to the list, but don't get impatient. That comes later. His response to God's grace in Jesus Christ is faith. "You just believe" is not the Eleventh Commandment, the one giving us a way to save ourselves. Faith is the gift God gives to us. When we hear the glorious Gospel of Christ, we become like the man some people called Doubting Thomas, but became best known when he became Believing Thomas and said to Jesus, "My Lord and my God!" (See John 20:28.) We do not say we understand. We do not say we know. Both our knowledge and our understanding are limited by our human condition. But God's grace has come to us from the outside, and our faith goes back to him beyond the limits of our comprehension.

We cannot make ourselves believe, and we cannot make others believe. When the first missionaries arrived in Iceland, they made the leaders of the local people stand in a line. They asked the first one if he believed in Jesus. He said, No!" The missionaries propped his mouth open and forced a live snake down his throat. The same thing happened to the second. Guess what! The third one believed in Jesus! Such a story is repulsive to us today. I do not tell the story to degrade those missionaries, that would be too easy. I tell the story to ask if we use political, social, family, or financial pressure instead of snakes to try to make people believe.

We need to teach people how to hear the Gospel. It is not a lesson in moral living; it is the power of God for salvation to all that believe. (See Romans 1:16.) Let people know that a miracle happens each time the Gospel reaches our minds and hearts. Teach them to listen for the Gospel, not as one paragraph in a sermon, not as the repetition of the things Jesus did, but as the power for all we are and all that we do. When they have heard the word of the Gospel, let them respond with joy, "I believe!"

CHAPTER 11

Let Me Illustrate My Illustrations

Baptism

Galatians 3:27. Imagine yourself all dressed up and about ready to leave for an important appointment when you spill some food on your shirt or blouse. The food makes a mess and you don't have time to change. But you are fortunate. Your jacket totally covered the soiled part of your shirt or blouse.

Paul tells us we are sinners—our lives have been soiled by our disobedience of God's Law. We can't change that. But he also tells us that when we were baptized, we put on Christ. Christ becomes the jacket the covers our sins. He covers our sin, not by hiding them, but by forgiving them.

Care

An Amelist

1 Peter 5:7. The word *theist* comes from a Greek word meaning a person who believes in a god. An *a* in front of a word negates it; so an atheist is one who does not believe in a god. *Gnostic* describes those who know. An *a* before it makes it agnostic—one who doesn't know if there is a god.

We may know a few atheists and a few agnostics. But those words do not seem to fit those of us who go to church regularly. Let me give you a new word. It's not in the dictionary or in your spell checker. The word is *melist*. Also from the Greek, it means one who cares. An *a* in front of it makes it an amelist—one who doesn't care. Sometimes we don't care about other people. Sometimes we don't care about God. In either case we become amelist.

Only faith can change the hearts of atheists and agnostics. Only love from Jesus Christ can change the hearts of amelists.

CHRIST

Christ in Our Lives

Show a large clock with the 12 numbers and hands that can be moved. At the beginning have the small hand under the large one so it cannot be seen. Move the hands together to illustrate that you cannot tell time by the clock with only one had. You must see both hands to know what time it is.

Now show another clock face with the following words in place of numbers. CHRIST is at the top. Other words can be used anywhere: LOVE, SIN, WORSHIP, PRAYER, DEATH, BAPTISM, CHURCH, LAW, FAITH, FEAR, HOPE. Again have the small hand hidden under the large one. Move the hands around to point to a few of the words. Briefly talk about the good or bad ideas we have about each topic. Then point the large hand to JESUS at the top. Move the small hand around to a few of the subjects. Notice that the two hands give us a different view. The small hand may point to sin, but when the large hand points to Christ, we remember our sins are forgiven. The small hand points to hope, but when the large hand points to Christ it shows us where we get our hope.

This idea may be used as a series of sermons by going into more detail on the variety of subjects. Other words may be used on the clock face to show how the presence of Christ alters their meanings. You must see both hands to see how Christ helps in all parts of your life.

The Humanity and Divinity of Christ

Romans 1:3–4. Ask people to join you in doing this. Look at the front of your hand. Now look at the back. You can easily see the difference between the front and back of your hand. Now hold your hand about 18 inches in front of your face at a right angle to your forehead. You can still see the front and back of your hand. Now slowly move the hand closer to your eyes. As the hand nears your eyes, you can no longer focus on the two sides. Both sides of the hand are still there, but your eyes can't figure them out.

Look at Jesus. You can see him as a human. Think of things that show that he is a real person like us. You can also see him as God. Think of things that show he is God. As long as we think of Jesus as one or the other, we can understand him. But trying to see him as God and human at the same time is like bringing the hand close to the eyes. Our minds cannot focus on Jesus as both God and human at the same time.

The Lamb of God

John 1:29. The sacrifice of lambs was a personal part of Jewish family life. The family raised their own lambs and would pick one lamb each year that would be used later for the Passover meal. That was a special lamb. Members of the family feed it and took care of it along with the other lambs. However, it was their lamb for the sacrifice. When they visited other people, they would also see other special lambs. The neighbor Jacob would say, "That is my lamb for the sacrifice." Their cousins would say, "There is our lamb." Speaking to people with that custom, John the Baptist pointed to Jesus and said, "There is God's Lamb who will take away the sins of the world."

Christ the Way

Take a look at the magazines for sale in a book store. There are magazines for every special interest group. Look across the rows: golfing, sewing, fishing, gardening, hunting, and woodworking. There are magazines for gun collectors, mechanics, skydivers, model makers, and history buffs. There are crossword puzzles, pornography, recipes, and lists of bed and breakfast places. There are magazines for those who use computers, go on diets, and collect stamps.

To some people, the message of the Gospel of Christ is just one more magazine in the rows for all the special interests the people have. If you like that sort of thing, it's okay for you. But Christ came as God's Son for all people—and for all of their needs. The Gospel is an article in each category of magazine named above and for all of those not named. Jesus came to destroy sin and death—two special interest groups that apply to all people.

Which Jesus?

In the headlines of today's world we often read of a variety of identifications for Christ. People put an adjective in front of his name to limit the view of him. Some refer to the historical Jesus. Others talk of the mystical Jesus. Others want the spiritual Jesus. I have two adjectives for my Savior. I believe in the crucified Jesus. I believe in the resurrected Jesus. And they are the same Jesus!

LIFE OF CHRIST

Birth

(During the week before the service, ask the parents of a newborn baby to record the child crying. Select a good crying section and have the audiocassette ready to play at that point.)

Luke 2:7. In the order of worship, list the reading of Luke 2:7. Then put:

"Baby's Sermon: (Give name of the baby on the audiocassette.)"

After Luke 2:7 has been read, allow for a short pause; then play the tape. Continue the reading of Luke 2.

Daily Life

Matthew 9:11. Because we believe that "birds of a feather flock together," we don't like to be seen with people who commit certain sins. Others might think we are like them. We need to stay away to show our innocence. Jesus didn't have that problem. He always hung out with sinners—even the publicly condemned variety. He didn't have to worry about his reputation because he knew he was holy. We have to worry about ours because we know we're not holy. But Jesus was willing to wear our feathers. He looked like us—like us sinners. By his death we can now look like him—like his holiness.

Resurrection

A Jewish college student explained why she sang in the school's annual presentation of Handel's *Messiah*. "In my head I don't believe in Jesus and am not too sure about God. But when I sing the 'Hallelujah Chorus,' I believe in my heart that Christ rose from the dead."

Ascension

When we relocate, we leave a forwarding address. When Jesus ascended from earth to heaven, he left a forwarding address. Remember he said, "I will be with you always." (Matthew 28:20) He was saying, "Send my mail to your place."

CHURCH

Commitment

Matthew 9:12. We often say that the church is not a rest home for saints, but it is a hospital for sinners. What kind of care do you want from the Church Hospital?

Some want outpatient treatment only.

Some want only emergency care.

Some want to use only the pediatrics wing.

Some want to use only the geriatrics wing.

Some want to wait for the church to give an autopsy.

Some want to be committed to the church—committed for lifelong treatment.

1 Corinthians 12:7. Via a video at a museum in Dover, England, an elderly man tells about his experiences as a teenager during the Dunkirk evacuation during World War II. He told how the people in their small town sent all of their children away to make room for the almost 300,000 soldiers they brought across the English Channel in their little boats. The local people divided the little food and medical care available with their guests. They gave up their homes to house the sick. Many people lived in the caves under the White Cliffs of Dover.

After the man had described all of the difficulties, he added, "That was the best time of my life. We all worked together because all of us were needed. There were no arguments about who should do what. We all had plenty to do. I was treated as a responsible adult—and I was one."

This is one of many stories that show how people work together when they share a common problem. Great tragedies bring out the best in most (not all) people. A question: What if we could work together, not because of a problem, but because of an opportunity? All of the people in Dover felt the need of the armies at Dunkirk. What if we all felt the need to share the Gospel of Christ with all other people? What if we felt the need to provide Christian education for people of all ages? What if we felt the need to help people with physical and emotional problems? Would working on those challenges bind us together like the people of Dover in World War II?

Look at your church bulletin. We are doing these things. If you are a part of these efforts, enjoy it and invite others to work with you. If you are not a part of it, look at these opportunities for you to do something worthwhile for others. With your help, we can do much more.

Forgiveness

John 20:23. Look at a check that comes from a business. Of course, it has a name of who gets the money and the amount to be paid. It also needs a signature to authorize the payment. The person who signs the check in the lower right hand corner is not paying the money. The money comes out of the account named in the upper right hand corner. The business has authorized someone to sign the check.

Think of forgiveness as a check. First see a check written to you. It pays for all sins. Who signs the check? Not Jesus. His name is in the upper left-hand corner. He is the one who made the deposit that pays for all sins. The person who told you about Christ's love and forgiveness signed the check because Jesus authorized those who believe in him to forgive others.

That means you can also sign a check on Jesus' account. When you sign the check, you do not pay for the sins of another person. Instead, you tell them that Christ has paid for them and that you have the right to forgive them in his name.

Sin Erased

Psalm 130:3. In the days of typewriters we had erasers and correction fluid to cover our mistakes. However, when the page was held to the light, the corrections could still be seen. When we correct a mistake on a computer, the printed page has no record of the error. It has been removed. When Christ forgives us, he removes our sin. It is not a part of his record of our lives. He doesn't cover our sin with correction fluid. He paid the price of the sin, and it is gone.

Again

Same message, different illustration:

Let me give you two illustrations of forgiveness. First, I make a big mark on this piece of paper. That is a sin. The sin is forgiven. Wad up the paper and throw it in a wastebasket. Rapidly repeat the action several times.

Now let me show you another example of forgiveness. With chalk or a marker make a mark on a board. Identify it as sin and erase it. Rapidly repeat the process several times. Which example of forgiveness do you like best? At first, they seem to be almost the same. But, look what I can do. Pick up the papers from the wastebasket and straighten them out. See how many times I forgave you! Count the papers. But we can't count the number of times that I forgave on the board. The evidence is gone. When Christ forgives us, the evidence of our sin is gone. There is no record.

Grace

Romans 5:2. What if there was only a limited amount of grace available? Think of the announcements that might be made in a worship service:

1. Because of a shortage of grace today, we can forgive only sins against the even-numbered commandments.

2. Unfortunately, we are short on grace today so only those who are seated on the left side of the church are forgiven.

3. We have used up our allotment of grace for this week, but we invite you to come back next Sunday with the hope that we have received a new supply.

It all sounds silly, doesn't it? And it is! God loves us so much that his grace through Jesus Christ has no limits and no expiration dates. Christ has died for you. All of your sins are forgiven.

LAW/GOSPEL

Old and New Natures

Galatians 5:19–26. Print SAINTS on one side of an athletic shirt and SINNERS on the other. Put the shirt in a box. Explain you are going to use a football game as an illustration for the text. One team in the game is called the SAINTS. (Hold up the shirt to show that side, then drop the shirt back in the box). The other team is the SINNERS. (Pick up the shirt but show the other side, then put it back into the box.) The problem with this game is that each play is on both sides. (Pick up the shirt again and show both sides.)

Use verses 19–21 of the text to explain our sinful nature that puts us on the SINNERS team. Then use verses 22–26 to show the Holy Spirit has called us to be on the SAINTS team. Ask the hearers to think of themselves on each team. Who coaches them as sinners? How do they score as sinners? How do they cheer for the sinners' team? Who cheers for them when they play as a sinner? Who coaches as saints? How do they score as saints? How do they cheer for the saints' team? Who cheers for them when they play as a saint?

Galatains 5:19–26. Like movies sermons can have sequels. The following is another illustration of the same text and message.

Preparation: Put red colored water in a large nontransparent bowl—a punch or industrial-sized mixing bowl will work. Place a smaller dish (perhaps a large measuring cup) filled with green water inside the large bowl. The smaller container should not be visible to the hearers. You also will need a ladle and a clear drinking glass.

Say that for this illustration red is bad—it means stop doing that. Green is good—it means keep on going. Our evil nature leads us to do many bad things. Dip from the red water and place it in the glass. Speak about the sins mentioned in verses 15–21 and identify them with the red water in the glass. Pour the water back with the red water in the bowl and explain that it is a part of our nature.

Now dip from the center dish and fill the same glass with green water. It will appear that the water is coming from the same dish. Use verses 22–26 and talk about what the Holy Spirit produces in our lives. The Spirit does these things through us. Because of Christ's grace, the good things have become a part of our lives. Pour the green water back with the green water in the dish.

It seems impossible that both green and red water could come from this dish—just as it seems impossible for us to be both sinners and saints. First, let me show you this. The bowl is filled with red water, but I added the green in this dish. The green and red are not mixed together, but both are in the bowl. By our sinful nature we are like the bowl—we are sinners. But by God's grace through Jesus Christ, the Holy Spirit has given us a new life. Our new life and our sinful nature are not mixed into one, but both exist in us. We do evil things. But by the power of the Spirit, we also have many spiritual gifts. We can use them to serve God and one another.

Fulfilled Law

Matthew 5:17. Let's look at God's Law in two ways:

First, think of it as something you must do. Here is an empty glass. Each time you obey the Law, you get to put one bean in the glass. Name several good things and put a number of beans in the glass. However, each time you do something wrong, or forget to do what you should do, you must take a bean out. Empty the glass. Many people look at God's Law this way. They go through life trying to fill their lives with good things, but the bad things wipe out the good.

Listen to what Jesus said in Matthew 5:25. Jesus knew we couldn't keep God's Law, but he didn't cancel that Law because we need it to protect ourselves from each other. So Jesus does something for us. He fulfills the Law. He makes it come true. Jesus didn't break God's Law by doing bad things, and he did all the good things that the Law required. His glass is full. Fill the glass. Then he gives us the full glass.

Instead of starting with an empty glass that we must fill, we start with a full glass. When we sin, we lose some of the beans. But we come back to Jesus when we repent of our sins, and we ask him to forgive us and fill the glass again.

Lord's Supper

1 Corinthians 10:16. A woman told about her spiritual search. Several times she was invited to the altar to receive Christ. Each time she got a handshake, a prayer, and a tract.

Then she went to a church that invited her forward to receive the Lord's Supper. "I went," she said, "and received Christ."

Matthew 26:26–28. When I'm hungry I won't want to talk or read about food. I don't want to look at pictures of food. I don't want to remember the meals I've eaten in the past or will eat in the distant future. When I'm hungry, I want food now.

When I am spiritually hungry, I don't want just to talk or read about Christ. I don't want to look at symbols. I don't need to hear what he did long ago or what he will do in heaven. I need Christ's presence. I need to receive his body and blood as he gave them to me.

PRAYER

Prayer as the Last Resort

An atheist on vacation in Scotland wanted to have a good story to tell his friends back home, so he rented a small boat and went sailing on the Loch Ness. Suddenly, a large monster surfaced nearby then dived under his boat. The waves caused the boat to pitch to the point of turning over.

"Help me, God! Help me!" the man pleaded.

"But five minutes ago you didn't believe in me," God answered.

"But five minutes ago I didn't believe in the Loch Ness Monster either," the man said.

Often people do not believe in God or in accidents, sickness, or death until they happen. When they see the problem is real, then they want God to be real.

1 Thessalonians 5:17. When God tells us to pray without ceasing, he doesn't mean for us to do nothing but pray. Instead, we should do nothing without prayer.

Prayer Stopwatch

Let me give you an imaginary stopwatch. This one works backwards. Instead of starting it to see how long an activity takes, you start this one to see how much time passed between an event and your response to God. Let me show you how it works. You receive bad news. You worry about it. You try to decide what to do. You do lots of other things. How long does it take you to pray? When you remember to pray, activate the stopwatch and figure out the time of delay between when you felt the problem and when you asked God for help.

You can also use this stopwatch this way. You receive good news. You are excited. You tell other people. You do all kinds of things, but how much time elapses before you thank God. When you do remember to thank God, use the stopwatch to measure the time between when you received the good news and the time you thanked God.

Keep this imaginary stopwatch with you at all times. It will be a good reminder that God is always waiting and ready to hear from you.

SIN

Abuse of God's Name

Jesus came close to a woman who had stood on the edge of Christianity most of her life. She became active in worship, service, and Bible study. During a discussion on the commandment on the use of God's name she said, "I hope I live long enough to invite as many people to heaven as I have told to go to hell."

In a group of men who worked together, one was an atheist, another a Christian, and the rest were somewhere in between. One day the atheist became angry with the Christian and cursed him. In a loud voice he damned the man to hell. The others were surprised that the Christian was not upset. But the Christian explained, "That guy doesn't believe in God. He has no authority to pronounce judgment in God's name. You've got to believe in God to be able to call on him to do anything. So I don't sweat his curses."

Bumper Sticker: "Be Different—Go to Heaven!"

Complaints

Numbers 11:5. When they were in the wilderness, the Israelites remembered the salad bars back in Egypt but forgot the brickyards.

Covetousness

God planned for us to love people and use things. We mess up his system when we love things and use people.

Gossip

In some Latin American countries gossip is called "Lip Radio."

Greed

When Cortez came to what is now Mexico, he told the natives, "The white man has a big sickness in his heart that can be eased only with gold."

Idolatry

Matthew 6:24. Sometimes we try to be bispiritual by serving two gods at one time. It never works because God is not in competition with the gods. God, by definition, is one. He is the one who created us and he is the one who has redeemed us.

Out of the Heart

Matthew 15:19. In our hearts we have many boxes that contain sin. Each of us seems to have special problems with certain sin boxes. Some always need to have their worry box full. As soon as they get rid of one worry, they fill the box with another. Some keep their anger box full all the time. If they lose one reason to be angry, they will find another. Some keep their greed box in constant use. As soon as they get one thing, they want another. Some have a box that is always full of lust, though they may frequently change the object of the lust. The list goes on because all sin comes out of the hearts and desires of people.

Christ came to fill those boxes with forgiveness, grace, and love. By his death for us, he emptied all of the boxes of their guilt. By his presence with us, he continues to help us in our struggle against the sins of our hearts by giving us the love of his heart.

Resurrection

For the grave marker of one who planned ahead:
Name: _____
Born: 1933
Died: _____
Will Rise: _____

Sovereignty

An employee of a small business always disagreed with the owner about the way the business should operate. Each time the boss gave instructions, the employee would give a minority opinion. He would explain to the other workers how the owner was making mistakes. He worried that the business would fail. He had all of the worries and headaches of being the owner without any of the responsibilities. He did not do his own work well because he was always trying to boss the boss.

Sometimes people try to be God's boss. They don't like the commandments God gave and would be glad to edit them. They like the idea of a Gospel for all people but think it's narrow-minded to believe the Gospel must be connected to Christ. They can't see why some people die young and why some old people don't die. These people would do their own job better if they would do the job God gave them and let God do his job.

Values

The British War Museum in London has recorded the experiences of many people during the air raids on London during World War II. One person made this observation: "I noticed after the war those who had lost loved ones during the air raids often became gentle and caring people; while those who lost most of their home and property became bitter and resentful."